THE NEW
ANSWER BOOK OF
SPORTS

By BILL MAZER

Answers to Hundreds of Questions about the World of Sports

Publishers • GROSSET & DUNLAP • New York

FOREWORD

There has already been so much said about how sports provides a common meeting ground for people of all ages that I'm not about to add even a word.

What I would like to say as a foreword is that my first literary effort was dedicated to my wife who, as I put it then, "allowed me the time to pursue my labor of love with limitless time."

This work belongs strictly to those wonderful young people who helped me fill air time on radio station WNBC in New York for four and a half years with their questions and answers. It may sound as corny as "thanks to those who made this possible." I'll risk that, because at least I know how true and with what amount of feeling the expression is made.

So here is another session of questions and answers done in the same spirit as that produced in my meetings with sports fans everywhere.

Please enjoy.

Bill Mazer

Picture Credits

CONTENTS

Abner Doubleday (1819–1893)

BASEBALL

Who Invented Baseball?

Do you know what the toughest question about baseball is? It's: "How was the game invented?"

There's no one answer—because nobody knows for sure!

In 1907 a special committee of officials was named to determine the origin of baseball—that is, to find out who the founder was and where the first game was played. After their "investigation," they decided that Abner Doubleday had laid out the first field and organized the first baseball game in Cooperstown, New York; sometime in 1839. For that reason Cooperstown was selected as the site for the Hall of Fame and Baseball Museum, which were opened in 1939—on the supposed

100th anniversary of baseball.

But that 1907 committee couldn't have been more off base. Later historians discovered that at the time Doubleday was thought to be inventing baseball in Cooperstown he was a cadet at West Point. Furthermore, there was doubt that he had ever even played the game!

So how did baseball start in our country? The best-informed opinion of the historians is that the sport evolved early in the 1800's from cricket and another English game, rounders, which used posts for bases and had a batter who punched the ball and was put out by being hit with the ball. There were variations of the game known as "Town Ball" and "New York Game."

Some of this confusion about the history of baseball—and the different kinds of baseball—is understandable. What American boy has grown up without playing some variation of baseball? Maybe it was stickball on a city street, where hitting a rubber ball the length of three manhole covers with a broom handle was a homer. Or maybe it was

The first league game in baseball was played between teams from New York and Boston on April 29, 1886. As shown in this illustration, the fielders did not wear gloves.

o'cat (one old cat) on an empty lot, with four players on a side and one base. Or softball, played with a softer ball than the one in use now, the kind that had an outside stitch. Softball was popular in my time because you didn't need gloves (equipment was scarce in the Depression days). When you had gloves, then you played "hard ball," as we called regular baseball. Now there are the well-organized, well-equipped Little Leagues, Babe Ruth Leagues, American Legion Leagues, etc., but I'll bet we had just as much fun in our pick-up games, without uniforms and adult supervision.

But getting back to history. While the name baseball began to be commonly used as early as the 1820's, there was still no standard form of the game until 1846. On this historians are in complete accord.

Who Deserves the Credit as the Creator of Modern Baseball?

He was a young surveyor by the name of Alexander Cartwright. A Knickerbocker Baseball Club was formed that year and Cartwright, a member, was given the job of laying out a diamond and devising the rules of play. Cartwright placed the bases ninety feet apart, set up the foul lines, settled on nine players to a team and three outs to an inning—and even three strikes to a batter! A rule was added that a base runner also could not be put out by throwing the ball at him.

The first game was played at Hoboken, New Jersey, on June 19, 1846, between the Knickerbockers and a team called the New York Nine. Cartwright was the umpire and, ironically, his team was trounced, 23-1!

Cartwright's involvement with baseball ended shortly afterward, but he had done his work well. His original contributions to the game were officially recognized when he was elected to the Hall of Fame.

Alexander Cartwright

Cartwright laid down the basic principles, but it took half a century—until nearly 1900—before baseball was played the way we know it today. Pitchers at first were allowed only to throw underhand (the pitcher's box was 46 feet from home plate then), then side-arm, then shoulder-high and finally, in 1884, overhand. The pitching distance was increased, too, until the present 60 feet 6 inches was established in 1893. And it wasn't until 1887 that a batter no longer could call for a high or low pitch! And at one time nine balls were needed to walk a batter, the number gradually decreasing until the four-ball rule was put in effect in 1889.

In the 1890's the custom of the umpire raising his right arm for a strike started.

Billy ("Dummy") Hoy, an outstanding outfielder who played for St. Louis, Cincinnati and Washington from 1888 to 1902, was a deaf mute. Since he couldn't hear the umpire's call when he was batting, the umpires began the arm gestures to tell him what the count was. The custom has prevailed.

As any player can tell you, the official scorer is an important man. He's the sole judge on hits and errors—and think of the many close plays that come up through a season! His decision can mean the difference between a no-hitter and a one-hitter! The scorer's rulings affect batting averages, fielding averages and earned-run averages, and these are the figures on which players negotiate next year's contract. In short, the scorer's decisions can touch a player in his most sensitive area—the pocketbook.

Every fan in the park looks to the scoreboard after one of those borderline hit-or-error cases to see which sign is flashed. But few fans know who the official scorer is and how he is chosen.

How Do You Score a Baseball Game?

Scoring a game is much like taking shorthand. There are probably many individual additions, but basically all scorers use the following system: the pitcher is listed as number one; the catcher, number two; the first baseman, three; the second baseman, four; the third baseman, five; the shortstop, six;

FIELDING			No.	NAME	Pos.	INNINGS													BATTING										
PO	A	E				1	2	3	4	5	6	7	8	9	10	11	12	AB	R	H	2B	3B	HR	RBI	SO	BB	SH	SB	HP
				BOSWELL	2b																								
				AGEE	cf																								
				GARRETT	3b																								
				JONES	lf																								
				SHAMSKY	rf																								
				KRANEPOOL	1b																								
				HARRELSON	ss																								
				GROTE	c																								
				SEAVER	p																								
				Totals		3/3																								

the leftfielder, seven; the centerfielder, eight; and the rightfielder, nine.

Indicating base hits is very individualized. Some scorers use dashes. I have always indicated them in this fashion: a single would be 1B; a double, 2B; a triple, 3B; a home run, HR. All scorers use the letter "K" to indicate a strike-out and "BB" for base on balls.

Tell you what—let's make up an inning of play and see what it looks like on the scorecard we have provided.

Who is Baseball's All-Time Greatest Ball Player?

Settling this one would give King Solomon headaches, but it has provided baseball fans with more enjoyable arguments than you can shake a bat at. Ty Cobb is baseball's all-time leading percentage hitter. He posted a career mark of .367 and led the American League in hitting twelve times. His running ability was about on a par with his hitting—sensational. However, he was just an average outfielder defensively. In contrast, Honus Wagner was a great hitter, a great runner and probably the greatest defensive short-stop of all time. Old-timers are almost unanimous in crediting him with being the perfect ballplayer.

One thing Honus didn't do was become an outstanding pitcher. Babe Ruth was that and more. Ruth's pitching ability was good enough to make him one of the best. But his home-run ability was better, so he became an outfielder, and a really good one. He could throw and field as well as anyone. His running too, though not spectacular, was better than average. And what a hitter! Experts have often said that Ruth could have hit for almost any average he wanted to, but the fans came to see him hit home runs and 714 times he didn't disappoint them.

If you think my vote goes to Babe Ruth, you're right.

Who Was Baseball's Last .400 Hitter?

Hall-of-Famer Ted Williams, who has just unretired himself to become a manager, turned the trick in 1941 when he batted .406. It should be noted that he refused to play it safe on the last day of the season. He was hitting .401 and could have sat out a double-header to insure staying above the rare .400 mark. But he insisted on playing and made six hits to raise his average to .406. Bill Terry of the New York Giants was the last National Leaguer to accomplish the feat with a .401 average in 1930.

Other players of note to bat .400 include Ty Cobb, on three occasions; Rogers Hornsby, also three times; Harry Heilmann; Joe Jackson; George Sisler (twice) and Napoleon Lajoie. These men hit over .400 from the year 1900 on. There were others who hit over .400 prior to 1900.

What is Considered Baseball's Greatest Record?

There may be debates in all areas of baseball, but there is almost complete agreement that Joe DiMaggio's 56-game hitting streak is the all-time record. How great it is is apparent when you realize that the best previous consecutive-game hitting record was set before 1900. In 1897, Wee Willie Keeler batted safely in 46 straight games. DiMaggio's hitting streak ended during a night game in Cleveland on July 17, 1941. Starting pitcher Al Smith and relief pitcher Jim Bagby, Jr. get the credit as pitchers of the game, but a third baseman named Ken Keltner made two spectacular plays in the field to "rob" DiMaggio of base hits.

Three of baseball's greatest "sluggers": (left) Babe Ruth hitting his sixtieth home run off Tom Zachary in 1927; (center) Ted Williams, formidable "long-ball" hitter of the Boston Red Sox; and (right) Bill Terry, last National Leaguer to bat over .400.

Who are the Nine Players Who Have Won the Triple Crown of Batting?

Ty Cobb of the Detroit Tigers was the first triple-crown winner in 1909. He hit .377, batted in 115 runs, and topped the league in homers with a grand total of nine. Heinie Zimmerman of the Chicago Cubs was the next one in 1912 with 14 homers, 98 RBI's, and an average of .372. Rogers Hornsby twice won the triple crown. He first swept the board in 1922, hitting 42 homers, batting in 152 runs with a .401 average. He repeated in 1925 with 39 homers, 143 RBI's and a .403 average.

After Hornsby's "double," two Philadelphia stars—Jimmy Foxx of the "A's" and Chuck Klein of the Phillies—did it in the same year, 1933. Foxx, batting .356, drove in 163 runs and rapped 48 four-baggers. Klein had 28 homers and 120 runs batted in with a .368 mark.

Lou Gehrig followed the next year with credentials of 49 homers, 165 RBI's and a .363 average.

Joe Medwick of the St. Louis Cardinals did the trick in 1937, getting 31

11

homers (tying him with Mel Ott of the Giants) and 154 runs batted in with a .374 average.

Ted Williams then did it twice. In 1942 he wrapped up his first triple crown with 36 homers, 137 runs batted in and an average of .356. He won his second in 1947, batting .343 as he stroked 32 four-baggers and drove in 114 runs. He and Hornsby are the only two players who have won batting's triple crown twice.

In 1956, Mickey Mantle of the Yankees had 52 homers, 130 RBI's and a 353 average.

Frank Robinson, playing for the Baltimore Orioles in 1966, hit 49 home runs and drove in 122 runs. His .316 batting average was the best in the league.

The next year Carl Yastrzemski become a triple crowner. His batting average was .326, his RBI's 121, and his home-run total, 44 (tying him with Harmon Killebrew of Minnesota).

How Many Players Have Hit Four Home Runs in a Single Game?

The number is ten. This exclusive list starts back on May 30, 1894, with Robert Lowe of Boston, who remains the only National Leaguer to clout his four in consecutive times at bat.

Ed Delahanty of Philadelphia was the next four-in-a-game hitter on July 13, 1896.

Then it took almost 36 years before Lou Gehrig did it on June 3, 1932, against the Athletics, in his first four trips to the plate. Gehrig nearly became the only player to wallop five, but Al Simmons raced deep into left field to haul down his long drive in the ninth inning.

Chuck Klein joined the club on July 10, 1936, although he needed ten innings to do it.

Twelve years later, Pat Seerey of the Chicago White Sox performed the deed on July 18, 1948; he needed eleven innings.

Gil Hodges of Brooklyn Dodgers was next, on August 31, 1950.

Joe Adcock of the Milwaukee Braves rapped his four on July 31, 1954. Rocky Colavito of the Cleveland Indians followed suit on June 10, 1959. Willy Mays of the San Francisco Giants did it on April 30, 1961.

And Mike Schmidt was the last player to do it, April 17, 1976. He did it in ten innings.

An interesting sidelight is that Billy Loes was a spectator at the Hodges, Adcock, Colavito and Mays four-homers-in-a-game feats, either on the same team as a hitter or on the opposing team!

Which Team Has Won the Most Pennants in Baseball?

If you said the New York Yankees, you are right. The Bronx Bombers have won 33 pennants. They are far ahead of any team in either league. The next closest team is a National League Team, The New York Giants, who won fifteen pennants from 1901 to the time they ceased to exist. If you count pre-1900, add two more to the Giant list.

In accumulating the 33 pennants the Yankees had the services of Miller Huggins for six of them, Joe McCarthy for eight, Bucky Harris for one, Casey Stengel for ten, Ralph Houk for three, Yogi Berra for one, Billy Martin for two, and Bob Lemon for two. The Yankees also have won the World Series more times than any other team. In their thirty-two appearances, they have come out on top twenty-two times.

Joe DiMaggio   Rogers Hornsby   Lou Gehrig

The New York Yankees, in 1939, coming out of their dugout before the start of another World Series championship.

What Players got Three Thousand or More Hits in Their Lifetimes?

Would you believe that up until 1969 only eight players had turned the trick? Since then, in a space of twelve years, seven more players have joined this illustrious list. They are: Ty Cobb—the only player with over four thousand hits. His total: 4,191. Then, in descending order, Henry Aaron, 3,771; Pete Rose, 3,697; Stan Musial, 3,630; Tris Speaker, 3,515; Honus Wagner, 3,430; Eddie Collins, 3,311; Carl Yastrzemski, 3,192; Adrian (Cap) Anson, 3081; Lou Brock, 3,023; Al Kaline, 3,007; and finally Roberto Clemente, 3,000.

Stan Musial, after smashing five homes in a double-header against the New York Giants on May 3, 1954.

Ty Cobb, pictured near the end of his career in 1928. The "Georgia Peach," as he was called, was considered the most dangerous base runner of all time.

Hack Wilson, who hit more home runs in one season than any other National Leaguer.

It is obvious that Pete Rose still has a few years remaining in his career and in spite of the baseball strike of 1981 he should become the second man to reach the 4,000 hit plateau. Whether he can break Cobb's all-time record is speculative but with Pete you never know. Rose is such a competitive human being that he can accomplish almost anything he sets his mind to. The biggest question is whether time can wither him.

Who Holds the Record for Most-Runs-Batted-In in a Season?

Lewis Robert (Hack) Wilson of the Chicago Cubs. His name may not mean much to this generation, but this roly-poly man drove in an unbelievable 190 runs in 1930. That same year he hit 56 home runs. The only man to approach this record was the immortal Lou Gehrig of the New York Yankees who owns the American League mark of 184 runs batted-in set in 1931. To get a greater appreciation of these statistics, there hasn't been a hitter who has batted in more than 159 runs (other than Wilson) in the history of the National League.

In the American League, Babe Ruth with 170, Gehrig with 174 and 175, and Hank Greenberg with 170 and 183, are the only hitters in that rare company. Lou Gehrig, Jimmy Foxx, and Babe Ruth, incidentally, batted in a hundred runs or more in a season thirteen times. Stan Musial and Willie Mays accomplished this ten times.

Who Holds the Record for Most Stolen Bases in a Season?

If you said Maury Wills, you're wrong . . . unless, of course you added the record since 1900. Because, believe it or not, someone named Harry Stovey, playing for Philadelphia, of the old American Association in 1888, stole 156 bases; and in 1891, Billy Hamilton, playing for Philadelphia of the National League, swiped 115. Wills' mark of 104 in 162 games is the modern record. The great Ty Cobb holds the American League record of 96.

When ballplayers are judged, one usually refers to the bat, the arm and the legs. Ty Cobb (the "Georgia Peach") is the all-time record holder in two categories. His .367 lifetime batting average seems as safe from being overtaken as his mark of 892 stolen bases. The Georgian was truly a peach.

By the way, if anyone asks you what the record is for most stolen bases in a game, the answer (post-1900) is six—accomplished by Eddie Collins of Philadelphia (American League). A former Dodger, Pete Reiser, set a unique record when he stole home seven times in 1946.

Have Two Men on the Same Team Hit 50 Home Runs in the Same Season?

It has happened only once. The Yankees' famous M & M boys, Mickey Mantle and Roger Maris, did it in 1961. That was the year Roger Maris hit 61 home runs to break Babe Ruth's record of 60. Mickey Mantle hit 54 that same year.

How great this accomplishment is, aside from the fact that it has happened only once, is more obvious when it is noted that only seven other players in the entire history of baseball have hit over 50 home runs in a season. The Babe did it four times. Jimmy Foxx, Willie Mays, Mickey Mantle and Ralph Kiner, twice. Maris, Hank Greenberg, Hack Wilson and Johnny Mize did it once.

When Roger Maris hit the record-breaking number 61 off Tracy Stallard, a Boston right-hander, the struggle in the stands to get the ball was for more

The "M&M" boys, Mickey Mantle (left) and Roger Maris (right).

than baseball sentiment. A Sacramento, California restaurant owner had offered $5,000 for the ball Maris hit—such was the excitement surrounding this event. Strangely enough, the fans did not exactly relish (nor did Maris) the breaking of Ruth's record. The fans themselves probably would have chosen Mantle for this favored role. Both Maris and Mantle retired the same year, Maris to a beer distributorship in Florida and Mantle to the restaurant business.

How Many Pitchers Have Won More Than Three Hundred Games?

Warren Spahn recently brought the list to 14. He joined Grover Cleveland Alexander, John Clarkson, James Galvin, Robert Moses Grove, Walter Johnson, Tim Keefe, Christy Mathewson, Charles Nichols, Eddie Plank, Charles Radbourne, Michael Welch, Early Wynn and Denton (Cy) Young. "Spahnie" chalked up 363 wins in 21 seasons to become the winningest left-hander in major-league history. In the process he won 20 or more games in 12 seasons. As great as that was, it was still a far cry from Cy Young's record of 511 wins compiled in 22 sessions.

If you're going to make comparisons, though, just remember that Walter Johnson won 416 games in 21 seasons with Washington, a team that earned for that city the label of "First in war, first, in peace, and last in the American League."

Warren Spahn   Denton (Cy) Young   Johnny Vander Meer

How Many Pitchers Have Hurled No-Hitters in Both Leagues?

Only two—Jim Bunning and Cy Young. Jim Bunning pitched his first for the Detroit Tigers against the Boston Red Sox on July 20, 1958. Then, when he went to the Philadelphia Phils in 1964, he threw his second no-hitter against the New York Mets on June 21, 1964—and made it a perfect game, too.

Cy Young no-hit Cincinnati of the National League, while pitching for Cleveland on Sept. 18, 1897, and then repeated against Philadelphia on May 5, 1904 while pitching for Boston. By a strange coincidence, his second no-hitter was also a perfect game. But it didn't end there for Young. He added a third no-hitter against the Yankees on June 30, 1908.

Young's three no-hitters stood alongside Bob Feller's as a record until the great Sandy Koufax posted four. The first for Koufax came against the New York Mets on June 30, 1962. His second, on May 11, 1963, came against the Giants. The third, on June 4, 1964, was against the Phillies. And the record-breaking fourth was on September 10, 1965, against the Chicago Cubs. It's hard to say that even this feat is the greatest effort in no-hit history. Many experts feel that when Johnny Vander Meer threw consecutive no-hitters, that was the greatest. Vander Meer, while pitching for Cincinnati in 1938, no-hit Boston on June 11, and four days later he throttled the Brooklyn Dodgers!

While on the subject of no-hitters, let's not overlook the fact that, in addition to Vander Meer, Allie Reynolds in a Yankee uniform and Virgil Trucks while pitching for Detroit also delivered two no-hitters in one season. Trucks did it in 1952 against Washington and the Yankees, while Reynolds did it in 1951 against Cleveland and Boston.

We mentioned Bob Feller fleetingly in connection with no-hitters, but he deserves more space than that. Feller is the only pitcher who threw a no-hitter on opening day on the way to making his total of three. And while we're taking note of "onlys," Alva (Bobo) Holloman is the only rookie making his first major-league start to have turned the no-hitter trick. It didn't help

Bob Feller

Sandy Koufax

much. Before the end of his first and last season in the big leagues, he had been farmed out.

In closing the subject of no-hitters, two other baseball feats deserve mention. Harvey Haddix of the Pittsburgh Pirates joined the list of all-time hard-luck pitchers on the night of May 26, 1959, when he mowed down the Milwaukee Braves one-two-three for 12 innings. The first hitter for the Braves got on base on an error in the 13th, and after a sacrifice and an intentional walk, Joe Adcock's double turned the no-hitter into a one-hit one-nothing, defeat. And how about this one: Jim Vaughn pitched a nine-inning no-hitter, but his mound opponent, Fred Toney, pitched a ten-inning no-hitter with one out in the 10th. Vaughn finally gave up a hit. Let me add a third. The great Babe Ruth one day started a ball game against Washington, but when the first man up got a base on balls, Ruth became so incensed at the umpire that he was thrown out of the game. He was relieved by pitcher Ernie Shore. The runner at first tried to steal second, but didn't make it, and was out. Shore then retired the next 26 men and was given credit for a perfect game!

How is a Pitcher's ERA Rated?

If a pitcher has an ERA (earned-run average) of 1.00, it means that he has allowed an average of one earned run for every nine innings he has pitched. To determine a pitcher's ERA, divide the total number of innings pitched by nine, and then divide that figure into the total number of earned runs charged to the pitcher.

The all-time major-league leader in lowest earned-run average among pitchers who have won more than two hundred games is Grover Cleveland Alexander. He takes honors with an ERA of 2.56 for 696 games. It's ironic that Alexander is remembered more for the fact that he came in to strike out Tony Lazzeri of the Yankees in the 1926 World Series while pitching for the St. Louis Cards.

While Alexander holds the lifetime ERA record, a little-known pitcher named Ferd Schupp holds the season record with an ERA of 0.90. Schupp's record, though, was based on only 140 innings. Next lowest is Bob Gibson, with 1.12 in 305 innings in 1968. Grover Alexander in 1915 had an ERA of 1.22 in 376 innings. (Incidentally, Hollywood once made a motion picture based on Alexander's life, and the actor who played the part of this all-time great pitcher was Ronald Reagan, who subsequently became President of the United States!)

Still in the ERA record category, Lefty Grove led his league nine times, the most by any pitcher, and only one pitcher led both leagues in ERA. Hoyt Wilhelm, pitching for the Giants in 1952, led the National League, and then, while with Baltimore, in the American League in 1959, earned the distinction of leading that league, too.

Who Struck Out the Most Men in a Lifetime?

Way out in front—as a matter of fact, the only pitcher in the three-thousand strike-out category—is the immortal Walter Johnson. This great, gentle human being used only one pitch, a fast ball . . . but *what* a fast ball! Al Schacht, known as the "clown prince of baseball," was a teammate of

Johnson's. On many occasions Al has said that if Johnson had just a little meanness in him, no one could have hit him.

It was of Johnson that the story was told concerning a player who once went to the bench after only two strikes. The umpire called him back to the plate, reminding him, "You've still got a strike coming." "No thanks," said the hitter. "That's all I want to see of him."

Years later, another fireballing right-hander, pitching in a pre-season game against the St. Louis Cardinals, brought the same reaction. He was from Van Meter, Iowa, and bore the name of Robert Feller. Rapid Robert set some fancy records in his time. One year he struck out 348 men. On October 2, 1938, he claimed 18 strike-outs in one afternoon.

There are those who insist that the baseball years Feller lost while in the service of his country would have been his greatest. One thing is certain: even without those years, he left quite a mark. It wasn't until a handsome young left-hander from the Flatbush section of Brooklyn appeared on the scene that Feller's name was erased at the top of the strike-out list for a season's play. That lefty—Sandy Koufax—notched 382 strike-outs in 1965 for the all-time record. In the entire history of baseball there have been only three pitchers to strike out more than three hundred men in a season: Bob Feller, Sandy Koufax and a colorful left-hander named Rube Waddell. Waddell struck out 343 men in 1904. Actually, though, even earlier—in 1886—there was a pitcher named Matthew Kilroy who struck out 505 men while pitching for Baltimore. Yes, Kilroy was there, but here's the catch: the distance from the pitcher's mound to the plate was only 50 feet. Today it's 60 feet 6 inches.

What Pitcher Broke a Record in 1968 That Had Lasted for 55 Years?

That pitcher was Don Drysdale of the Los Angeles Dodgers. Don pitched 58 consecutive shut-out innings to break the 56 mark Walter Johnson had set back in 1913. Drysdale actually broke another mark along the way that was of even longer duration—he pitched six consecutive shut-out games. The old record was five, recorded in 1904 by G. Harris White. For Drysdale this record had to be the highlight of his career. Johnson, however, still holds first place in the lifetime shut-out circle—he is the only man to have recorded more than a hundred shut-outs in a lifetime. The total comes to 113.

Don Drysdale

What is Considered the Greatest Game Ever Pitched?

You would get arguments here, but if you feel that the World Series is the time when clutch performers really come to the front, then Don Larsen's masterpiece for the Yankees in the fifth game of the 1956 World Series gets the nod. Sal Maglie started for the Brooklyn Dodgers, and he had a perfect game going, too—until the fourth inning. With one out, Mickey Mantle smacked a homer. That was all Larsen needed, but the Yankees got him another run in the seventh and Maglie wound up pitching a five-hitter, normally a winning effort. Larsen, who had been shelled off the mound in the second inning of the second game, was so superb in his control that only one hitter—Pee Wee Reese, in the first inning—carried the count to three balls. In all, Larsen threw only 97 pitches. In the ninth inning, with two out and 64,519 fans in Yankee Stadium holding their breath, Dale Mitchell was sent into pinch-hit for Sal Maglie. With the count one ball, two strikes, Mitchell fouled off the next pitch. Then Larsen, using his "no wind-up" delivery, threw another fast ball. Mitchell started to swing, stopped—and Umpire Babe Pinelli, working behind the plate in his last World Series before retiring, called strike three. Twenty-seven men up, 27 men down. Larsen had carved out a special niche in World Series history, the only man to pitch a perfect game.

Sequence pictures showing the pitching form of Don Larsen.

Only seven other men have pitched perfect games since 1900. In that exclusive list we find Cy Young, Boston vs. Philadelphia (AL), in 1904; Adrian Joss, Cleveland vs. Chicago (AL), in 1908; Ernie Shore, Boston vs. Washington (AL), in 1917; C. C. Robertson, Chicago vs. Detroit (AL), in 1922; James Bunning, Philadelphia vs. New York (NL) in 1964; Sandy Koufax, Los Angeles vs. Chicago (NL), in 1965; and Jim (Catfish) Hunter, Oakland vs. Minnesota (AL), in 1968.

Who Almost Pitched a No-Hitter in a World Series?

Floyd Bevens was the Yankee pitcher who came too close to baseball immortality. Although he had been wild, putting himself in trouble often, Bevens had silenced the Brooklyn bats for eight innings. Two of the many bases on balls he issued had paved the way for a Brooklyn run in the fifth. The Yankees, however, had scored twice, so that Bevens was protecting a 2-1 lead as well as striving for the no-hitter as the last of the ninth opened.

Bruce Edwards, the lead-off batter, flied out. Bevens then gave up his ninth walk to Carl Furillo. Spider Jorgensen popped out in foul territory to George McQuinn. Only one out to go! But Al Gionfriddo, a pinch-runner for Furillo, swiped second, running as Brooklyn had throughout the Series on Yogi Berra, who was then inexperienced behind the plate. Pete Reiser, who

23

had an injured leg, was batting for Hugh Casey. With first base now empty, Yankee manager Bucky Harris ordered an intentional pass to Reiser, which meant the winning run was on base.

Eddie Stanky was up next. Even though the second baseman was a sharp-eyed batter, the Dodger mastermind, Burt Shotton, pulled a surprise by sending up another right-handed swinger, veteran Harry ("Cookie") Lavagetto. Cookie banged a double off the right-field wall, scoring the two runners, and not only did Bevens see his no-hit masterpiece demolished, but he also lost the game, 3-2. The pinch two-bagger proved to be Lavagetto's only safety of the Series. The luckless Bevens was left with a dubious entry in the record book—most walks by a pitcher, 10.

Has Only One Left Hander Won Three Games in a World Series?

The answer is no. Believe it or not up until 1968, only one lefty had won three games in a World Series. That was Harry ("The Cat") Brecheen. Pitching for the St. Louis Cardinals against the Boston Red Sox in the 1946 World Series, Brecheen won three games. Even Whitey Ford, the winningest pitcher in World Series history, and Sandy Koufax, as well as Bob Grove couldn't do it. Then in 1968, Mickey Lolick did it. Interestingly enough, the Detroit left hander beat the St. Louis Cardinals three times. There are plenty of right handers who have won three games in one series. Christy Mathewson of The New York Giants and Jack Coombs of the Philadelphia Athletics turned the trick in only a five-game series—Matty in 1905 and Coombs in 1910. Urban Faber won three in a six-game World Series for the Chicago White Sox in 1917. In a seven-game series, Babe Adams of Pittsburgh in 1909, Stan Coveleski of Cleveland in 1920, Lew Burdette of Milwaukee in 1957, and Bob Gibson of the 1967 St. Louis Cardinals are the standard-bearers. There are three pitchers who did it when the series went to eight games. Deacon Phillippe of Pittsburgh and Bill Dinneen of Boston did it in 1903, and Smokey Joe Wood produced three wins for Boston in 1912.

24

Did Babe Ruth Ever Pitch in a World Series?

And how! The Babe won three games and never lost one in his World Series appearances as a pitcher. He was involved in the longest game won by a World Series pitcher. In 1916, the Babe outpitched Sherry Smith of Brooklyn and gave Boston a 2-1 victory. More than that, until Whitey Ford came along to break it, Ruth held the record for consecutive scoreless innings in World Series play. The Babe pitched 29 of them. Ford (another lefty) erased the mark by extending the streak to 33⅔ innings before he was scored on by wonderful Willie Mays.

We started this by talking about Babe Ruth. He holds one World Series record that may never be broken. He got ten hits—including three doubles and three homers in sixteen times at bat—in the 1928 Series for a .625 batting average as the Yanks swept the St. Louis Cardinals in four games.

Which Pitcher Holds the Record for Most Strike-Outs in a World Series Game?

If you said Bob Gibson, you are right. This superb right-hander, who was a good-enough basketball player to be a member of the Harlem Globetrotters, took the Sandy Koufax record of 15 off the books in the first game of the 1968 World Series. The background for the game was really unusual. Gibson had had an outstanding year, winning 22 and losing 9 with a 1.12 ERA. But even

Whitey Ford

Bob Gibson

Catcher Yogi Berra

these accomplishments were over-shadowed by his mound opponent, Denny McLain. McLain had done something no pitcher had done in 37 years—he had won 31 games. Faced with this challenge, Gibson rose to the occasion like the true champion he is. He bested McLain and the Detroit Tigers, 4-0, and en route struck out 17 men. Bob actually set another strike-out record: his total of 35 strike-outs is the most ever in one series.

The record for most strike-outs by one pitcher for total World Series is held by Whitey Ford of the Yankees at 94. You might have noticed by now that Whitey Ford's name appears quite a few times when one gets into World Series pitching records. Just checking it out, you realize that if there's such a thing as a World Series pitcher, it's gotta be Whitey. Here are his records: most World Series (11), most World Series games (22), most wins (10), most losses (8), most innings pitched (146), most bases on balls (34), along with the aforementioned most strikeouts in total World Series and most consecutive scoreless innings. What makes Whitey's records seem tough to break is that it doesn't seem likely that another team could so dominate a league as the Yankees once did, and so another pitcher may never get the chances Whitey had. And it's not only a matter of pitchers, but in other categories, too. For example, there's Yogi Berra, who has been in 14 World Series as a player. Yogi was on ten winners, went to bat 259 times, got 71 hits, 49 of them singles (a record). But all of this took place when the big question was, "Who's going to play the Yankees in the World Series?" Since no team is likely to repeat the Yankee successes, no ball player would get the chance.

26

What Was Bobby Thomson's "Shot Heard Round the World"?

Even if you weren't around in 1951, you may have heard of baseball's "shot heard around the world." It happened this way. The New York Giants, managed by Leo Durocher, had staged a "miracle" comeback to tie the Brooklyn Dodgers for the pennant. Now there had to be a play-off—best two of three games. The Giants won the first, 3-1. Back came the Dodgers to win the second, 10-0. It was all on the line that fateful day at the Polo Grounds. Going to the bottom of the ninth inning, it was 4-1 in favor of the Dodgers. Forgotten was the fact that the Brooklyns had blown a thirteen-and-a-half game lead they had in August. All big Don Newcombe, the Dodgers ace right-hander, had to do was get three men. You could hear the Dodger fans in the Polo Grounds screaming, "Get 'em, Newk!"

First up for the Giants in the bottom half of the ninth was Alvin Dark. He got an infield hit. When Don ("Mandrake") Mueller singled, putting runners on first and third, the Giant fans began to roar. Monte Irvin popped up

. . . and things quieted down. But not for long. Whitey Lockman doubled, driving in Dark and making the score 4-2. On the play Mueller sprained his ankle sliding into third and had to be carried off the field. Clint Hartung (The Hondo Hurricane) went in as a pinch-runner. Dodger manager Chuck Dressen then made the decision to bring in Ralph Branca, in relief of Newcombe. Up to bat came Bobby Thomson, the Staten Island Scot, as he was called. The issue wasn't in doubt long. Branca got his first pitch for a strike. His sec-

Bobby Thomson hitting the homer that won the final play-off game (and the National League pennant) in 1951 against the Brooklyn Dodgers.

ond pitch resulted in "the shot heard round the world." Thomson hit the shot into the left-field stands for a three-run homer that won the game, 5-4.

As you might expect, there were some who thought Dodger manager Dressen should have walked Thomson to get at the next hitter. But Chuck had simply followed the book: never put the winning run on base. Incidentally, the batter on deck for the Giants that day was their rookie centerfielder, a fellow named Willie Mays.

Who Inaugurated the All-Star Game?

The All-Star Game was the brainchild of Arch Ward, sports editor of the *Chicago Tribune*, who conceived of such a game in 1933. It has since become one of the major annual attractions of baseball. There was no game in 1945 because of governmental (wartime) restrictions on traveling. Two All-Star Games were played in 1959, and this practice continued through 1962; then the majors returned to a single game in 1963. At first, the stars to represent the American and National League were selected by a vote of the fans, but this system was abandoned in favor of having the players chosen by league executives and managers. Voting by fans was resumed in 1947, but again abandoned, and players, coaches and managers became the selectors. Two men who have seen most service in All-Star Games were Stan Musial for the National League, who participated in 24 games, and Ted Williams for the American League, who appeared in 18 games. These two players combined eminence with longevity. As a matter of fact, Ted Williams, Early Wynn and Mickey Vernon share the distinction of having played in the 1930's, 40's, 50's and 60's. The highest batting average produced by players with at least 20 at-bats in All-Star Games is a .500 mark for Charles Gehringer of the American League and a .433 average for Billie Herman of the National League. Both were second basemen. You're probably wondering, "What about Willie Mays?" Some say that wonderful Willie is the greatest all-star participant of them all. Through 1968, Willie had the most hits, 23, and the

Willie Mays sends a shot to the stands.

Carl Hubbell, master of the screwball.

most stolen bases, 6. He also had scored the most runs, 19. It is doubtful that anyone, including Arch Ward, foresaw the quality of baseball that was to flow at these games, particularly in those early days when the American League dominated the Nationals. With a Lefty Gomez perennially winning under an umbrella of support provided by the likes of Babe Ruth (who hit a home run in the first game) and other assorted American League sluggers, it looked as if the National League would never catch up—but it did. There have been so many heroes, one is almost unwilling to name them, for fear of leaving someone out. But let's march on fearlessly. Gomez and Ruth and Hubbell. And how, Hubbell!

It was the second game played in all-star competition. (The date—July 10, 1934.) On the mound for the National League was the Oklahoma southpaw. The arm which looked pretzel-twisted from throwing so many screwballs belonged to Carl Hubbell. There was no hint of the superlative feat that was to come from the way in which Hubbell started. Charlie Gehringer opened the game with a sharp single. Hubbell then walked Heinie Manush. Two men on, nobody out, and Babe Ruth at the plate. The crooked arm flailed the air and Ruth struck out on three pitches. "Iron Man" Lou Gehrig was next. He went down swinging. The Maryland strongboy, Jimmy Foxx, then dug in at the plate and became the third strike-out victim. More to come. Al Simmons, "foot-in-the-bucket" Simmons, led off for the American League in the second and whiffed. Joe Cronin became victim number 5. Bill Dickey then broke the spell and lined a single. Lefty Gomez, the gay caballero—admittedly not much of a hitter, even for a pitcher—quickly became strike-out number 6 as Hubbell wrapped up the finest two innings of mound work in All-Star history.

Then there was a July 8 game in 1941, with the American League down by two runs in the bottom of the ninth inning. A young splinter—they called him the "splendid splinter"—came to the plate and hit a towering home run to win the game for the American League. His name was Ted Williams, and the mark of greatness was on him, even at that young age. He was all of 22, and would go on that year to become a .400 hitter—.406, to be exact.

Then there was the seventeenth game of the series played by the all-stars, the one at Chicago that went 14 innings. It occurred on July 11, 1950, and the man who once managed the St. Louis Cardinals, Red Schoendienst, hit one into the seats to win it. That was the one in which Ralph Kiner (now a sports announcer) tied it up in the ninth for the National League. Earlier, in the first inning, Kiner had smashed a ball to left field that Ted Williams pulled down running into the wall. X-ray photographs taken the following day disclosed that Williams had suffered a fracture of the left elbow. Despite the pain, he had continued to play until the ninth inning, when he singled in a run to give the American League a short-lived 3-to-2 lead. That's quality that makes the difference.

Don't get the idea that all the good games were played long ago. In 1967—on another July 11, coincidentally, but this time in Anaheim, California—they played for 15 minutes before the National League won it 2 to 1. Don Drysdale and Jim ("Catfish") Hunter were the pitchers of record, Drysdale getting the win and Hunter the loss. A year later Drysdale was to set the all-time record for consecutive shut-out innings at 58 and Hunter was to become one of the select few who have pitched a perfect game.

And so it goes. The list is so long that to have named just a handful may seem unjust. I feel somewhat like a man who has been granted three wishes by a genie, and now that I've taken them, I just wish I had more. But for those whose deeds have gone unrecorded here, there is the consolation that their fans will always remember them. They were all great. They were *all* All-Stars.

Why is 1981 the Most Unique Year in Baseball History?

Because 1981 was the year of the longest strike in baseball history. There were times during the year when the game itself seemed in danger of never being played again as we know it. There was more talk about Marvin Miller—the players' representative and Ray Greeby—the owners' representative—than about anything else in baseball. So bitter and so intense was the feeling engendered by the strike that it may take years for its full impact to be overcome. On the surface the issue seemed to be the question of "free agentry". That is, a ball player's right to play out his contract and be picked up by another team without a penalty of some form being assessed against the team he left. Later there emerged the larger issue of cable television and the revenues derived from it. That may one day prove to be another issue to war over. When the strike was settled, two months of the season were lost and a new format introduced. A first season (before the strike) winner and a second season (after the strike) winner. The results were mini-playoffs that involved first half and second half winners. Lost in the shuffle was the Cincinnati team with the best record in baseball and no playoff spot. They had finished a half game back in the first season and a game back in the second season. Their fate seemed most to epitomize the injustice that swept baseball in the wake of "the great strike". It was indeed the most unique year in baseball.

Action during the Lehigh-Lafayette game in 1889.

FOOTBALL

Who Invented Football?

For younger readers, something should be made clear. Football was not invented by Joe Namath on January 12, 1969 at the Orange Bowl in Miami. True, "Broadway Joe" left an indelible mark on the game that day as he led his teammates to the first American League victory in the Super Bowl. In the afterglow of the upset win, Namath was credited with everything. But no, he did not invent football. As a matter of fact, deciding who invented football is something like deciding who invented baseball, except that football never was involved with a Doubleday myth.

Like baseball, football springs from English roots—soccer, or association football, and rugby. Soccer actually did not originate in England. In one form or another, that game has been played for several thousand years. Rugby, the historians tell us, is an English game. It originated accidentally in 1823 when William Ellis, a student at Rugby College, was involved in an interclass football (soccer) game. In those days one could only kick the ball. Ellis, a bit unhappy with his play, picked up the ball and ran with it. He received a great deal of criticism for this rash act, but when word spread regarding what he had done, some players felt that running as well as kicking would make the game a better one . . . and so, rugby came into being. There are some historians, notably Professor H. A. Giles, who assert that a game of football was played by the Chinese sometime from 300 B.C. to A.D. 500. In ancient Greece, a football game called Harpaston was popular.

The game as we know it today had its beginnings in 1869. That was the year Rutgers and Princeton pioneered intercollegiate football at New Brunswick, New Jersey, playing games on successive Saturdays, November 6 and November 13. Rutgers won the first, 6 to 4, and Princeton won the second, 8 to 0. After that came the deluge of football.

When Was the Forward Pass First Introduced to Football?

Historians have excavated an account of how the first forward pass came into being in a story of the Yale-Princeton game of November 30, 1876. The brief mention indicated that the ball was thrown forward after a player with possession had been tackled.

Another account of a game between the same rivals in 1883 indicated that the ball was thrown 25 feet after it was snapped from center. Thus, perhaps, grew the concept of the modern forward pass.

The next incident of a forward pass took place in Georgia-North Carolina game in 1895. The Carolina fullback got the ball and was undecided what to do with it. The Georgia players expected a kick and rushed the fullback, who had instructions to get rid of the ball fast, as far down field as possible. He took a few steps to one side and threw a short distance forward to one of the players, who went 70 yards for a touchdown.

Whenever the first forward pass was thrown, it was obviously a long time ago, and how it happened is an academic question. The passing attack as we know it today was perfected by two men, Charlie ("Gus") Dorais, the passer, and Knute Rockne, the No. 1 receiver, on the 1912–13 Notre Dame teams.

In 1913, against Army at West Point, they introduced the passing attack to the East. Dorais threw 21 passes and completed 17 of them for 243 yards. The wide-open style of attack, which gained big yardage, baffled the cadets who had expected an old-fashioned, line-smashing game. The Irish won, 35 to 13, with all five touchdowns being set up or scored on passes.

Knute Rockne showing a Notre Dame player how to block an opponent.

Is O.J. Simpson the Greatest Runner of Them All?

Answering this question is like deciding whether atheletes today are as good or better than the old-timers. If you think the old-timers were better, then you'll start throwing names like Willie Heston, Jim Thorpe, Ernie Nevers, Red Grange, Tom Harmon, Glenn Davis and Doc Blanchard at those who are for O. J. About the soundest argument I've heard is the one that says that great athletes are great in their time, and to compare athletes of different eras just doesn't make sense. It's tough enough making comparisons of athletes of the same era. For example, do you think that O. J. is a better runner than Gale Sayers or Jimmy Brown? If you're one of those "figure filberts," and that's the basis for your arguments, then you've got a strong case for O. J.

Gale Sayers

Fullback Jimmy Brown (32) gets the handoff and heads for a 65-yard touchdown run.

The great Southern California back ran for more yardage in just two years of major college ball (he had one year of junior college) than all but five men in football history. In 1968, he ran for 1,709 yards a single-season record for yards gained rushing. That, plus his 1,415 yards gained the previous year, gave him a grand total of 3,124 yards gained in just two years, by far the most yardage ever gained in two years. That total placed him sixth on the all-time rushing list, a list that included some who had gained their yardage in four years of play.

O. J.'s size (six feet two, 210 pounds) plus his blazing speed (9.3 in track competition) made him ideally suited for his job. Add to that his great balance and broken-field agility, and the picture is complete. If there was ever a man perfectly made for running, it's O. J. Simpson.

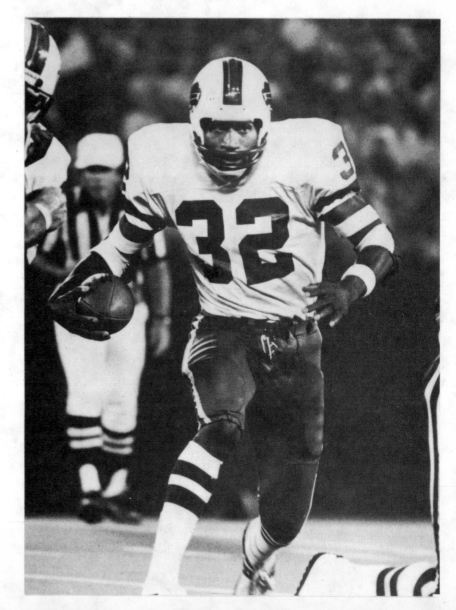

O.J. Simpson—The Man with the Golden Legs

Roy Riegels, seated on the ground, is disconsolate after his "wrong-way" run at the Rose Bowl on January 1, 1929.

Who Was "Wrong Way" Riegels?

Roy Riegels was the center and captain of the University of California Golden Bears, and he was involved in one of those episodes that have become football legend. It all happened in the Rose Bowl game of 1929, and seventy thousand fans in the stands witnessed it. In the second quarter, Riegels picked up a Georgia Tech fumble and started toward the Tech goal line. A platoon of Tech players sprung up around Riegels, and in trying to get away from them he cut back across the field. He apparently became confused and started toward his own goal line, 60 yards away. Players from both teams stood amazed as he ran down the sidelines. Benny Lom, a halfback for California, took off after Riegels, who turned on more speed as he heard footsteps behind him. Finally, the speedier Lom caught him, but not before he had gotten to the three-yard line—*his own* three-yard line! He was tackled there by a swarm of Georgian Tech players. California went into punt formation. The kick was blocked and Georgia Tech got a safety, which proved to be the difference, as they won the ball game, 8-7.

The famed Four Horsemen of Notre Dame: (left to right) Harry Stuhldreher, Don Miller, Jim Crowley and Elmer Layden.

How Did the "Four Horsemen" Term Originate?

Grantland Rice, one of the greatest sports writers ever, coined the phrase in 1924 when Notre Dame defeated Army, 13-7, before 55,000 spectators at the Polo Grounds in New York. What Rice wrote in his lead has become sports-writing literature—words many present-day sports writers wish they had written. This was Rice's lead paragraph:

"Outlined against a blue-gray October sky, the Four Horsemen rode again. In dramatic lore they are known as Famine, Pestilence, Destruction and Death. These are only aliases. Their real names are Stuhldreher, Miller, Crowley and Layden. They formed the crest of the South Bend cyclone before which another fighting Army football team was swept over the precipice at the Polo Grounds yesterday afternoon . . ."

Rice later wrote that the idea for the phrase had been planted in his mind a year earlier when Army played Notre Dame at Ebbets Field in Brooklyn. Rice watched the game from the sidelines because he only had a sidelines pass. On one wild end run the whole Notre Dame backfield swarmed over the sidelines where Rice was standing. The Irish backs swept right through Rice, who had fallen to his knees. "It's worse than a cavalry charge," he said to a friend. "They're like a wild-horse stampede!" The thought occurred to him again the next year in the press box at the Polo Grounds and he ticked it off on his typewriter. That's how the phrase "Four Horsemen" was born.

Glenn Davis (left) and Felix Blanchard (right), "Mr. Outside" and "Mr. Inside," respectively.

Felix ("Doc") Blanchard, running in the clear.

Who Were Mr. Inside and Mr. Outside?

Felix ("Doc") Blanchard and Glenn Davis. Blanchard played fullback and Davis halfback for the Army teams from 1944 to 1946. These two young men ran roughshod over opponents for three years. In 1944, the Cadets went undefeated in nine games, scoring an astounding total of 504 points against only 35. Entering their last college game against Navy in 1946, Blanchard, whose power enabled him to carry would-be tacklers along with him, and Davis, a swift, elusive runner, had engineered the Army teams to a three-year record of 26 wins and a tie against Notre Dame. They were also known as the Touchdown Twins.

Who Once Made Four Long Touchdown Runs in the First Ten Minutes?

Harold ("Red") Grange, the "Galloping Ghost" of Illinois, turned in one of the most memorable performances ever seen on a football field against Michigan at Urbana, Illinois, on October 18, 1924.

The flashing red-haired "pheenom" had been named an All-American the year before. He thrilled a crowd of 67,000 in single-handedly routing the Wolverines, 39-14.

39

(Left) Harold ("Red") Grange, the immortal "77" at the University of Illinois. (Above) Bronko Nagurski, all-time football great.

On the opening kick-off, Grange tore through the Michigan team for 95 yards and a touchdown. The game was little more than ten seconds old. Before the Wolverines could recover from the shock, Grange had galloped for 66, 55, and 40 yards. He even had time to leave to a thunderous ovation before the first quarter was over. He returned in the third quarter and scored a fifth touchdown on a fifteen-yard run, and in the fourth quarter he passed 23 yards for the last Illinois score. In all, he handled the ball 21 times and gained 402 yards. Grange was a baffling-type runner who could untangle himself from clusters of would-be tacklers when it seemed that he was hopelessly trapped.

As great as he was, he was virtually unknown in the East. Unknown, that is, until he hit Philadelphia on October 31, 1925 to play against the University of Pennsylvania. Grange proved that he was no myth. He slipped and twisted and turned from tacklers for three touchdowns as the Illini humbled Penn 24-2. Twice he went 60 yards for scores, and on his third touchdown he went 24 tough yards. In all, he gained 363 yards. The "Galloping Ghost" had done it again.

40

Whom Did They Call "Bronko?"

There may have been others who were called Bronko, but when you say that name and you mean football, there was only one, Bronko Nagurski. They tell the story that when "Doc" Spears, the Minnesota coach, found him, Nagurski was a raw-boned farm boy. Spears was trying to get directions to Duluth. "Which way to Duluth?" Spears is supposed to have yelled. The boy on the farm pointed—with his plow. Before he was through, Nagurski had pointed the way for the University of Minnesota and for the Chicago Bears. "The Bronk" was really unbelievable. It's sometimes hard to separate fact from fiction about him. One year he sustained an injury to his back, and since he couldn't bend over to play fullback, they put him on the line as tackle. He was just as good. When he bucked the line, it stayed bucked. For many years the record for most yards gained in the National Football League was held by a halfback named Beattie Feathers. He played for the Chicago Bears, running behind the blocking of Bronko Nagurski. Coach Jeff Cravath of Rice once said, "Eleven Nagurskis would wreck any other one-man team." It should be mentioned about the Bronk that he started as an end, switched to tackle and made All-American—and then switched to fullback and made All-American. They said of him that he ran his own interference. He was a rare one.

What Football Player Became a Justice of the U.S. Supreme Court?

A really great one named Whizzer White. He could do it all on a football field. He played for the University of Colorado where he had gone on an academic rather than a football scholarship. In 1937, Whizzer put Colorado on the football map. He led the country in scoring, rushing, and total offense. He was a fast shifty runner, strong enough to run over you if he had to. And in those days, when you had to play both ways, he did. He was a tremendous punter and he kicked extra points and field goals. They tell the story about how Whizzer, who once had just made a fine run, thought that the official

Byron ("Whizzer") White, pictured in 1937 as a star football player at the University of Colorado. He became a Rhodes scholar and a pro football star in later days—and eventually became an associate justice on the U.S. Supreme Court.

had called a play wrong. He said something about it to the official and it cost his team fifteen yards. There was another penalty called against the Colorado team and it backed them up almost to their goal line. But Whizzer took the ball on several running plays and led his team to a score.

As had been the case with Red Grange years before, White's exploits were viewed with doubt in the East. The experts figured that here was a good local boy. Well, Whizzer had his chance to prove his merit when Colorado played in the Cotton Bowl against a fine Rice team that was the champion of the Southwest Conference. Although the Colorado team wasn't the equal of the Rice eleven, White ran for one TD and passed for another. There was no doubt now about how good he was.

And so it was that the Pittsburgh Steelers offered him a chance in the N.F.L. White, though, had been named a Rhodes scholar and it didn't look like he could play pro ball (shades of Bill Bradley). But the Steelers finally convinced him and he played. He led the National League in rushing with a total of 567 yards. Later he played for Detroit Lions and made All-League. When John F. Kennedy became President of the United States, he named Whizzer White to the Supreme Court.

Who Was the Greatest All-Around Player?

This is the easiest way to start a real argument, but if there was a better all-around player than Jim Thorpe, he's been in hiding. What couldn't Thorpe do? Well, let's first talk about what he *could* do. He kicked the ball 80 yards with some frequency. Some old-timers insist they saw him kick it a hundred yards. He could drop kick the football as pretty as you please. And if you wanted, he could kick off. On defense he'd hit you and you might think that you'd been hit by a truck. The same held true for his blocking. Passing was one of those little-used things when he played. But if you played with a football, he could do anything with the ball. Yes, he could pass. Not like Joe Namath, but he could pass. He could catch. And he could run! Remember, this was the man who won the decathlon in the Olympics. Sure, they took his medals away from him because he played some semi-pro baseball, but they couldn't take away what the King of Sweden had said when he gave him those medals in 1912. "You sir," the monarch said, "are the greatest athlete in the world." And when that greatest athlete in the world took the pigskin in his hand and decided to run with it, he was something to behold. The story is told that when he played against someone who hit extra hard, he'd say, "Don't do that to Old Jim." If the opposing played didn't take heed, the big Indian would run over him so hard that the man would have to be carried off the field. That's how hard he ran. And if he wanted to, he'd give you all the fancy stuff, too. The swivel hip, the cut back, the stop and go, the change of pace. They were part of his equipment. He was, as the King of Sweden said, "the greatest athlete in the world."

Jim Thorpe, considered to be the greatest football player who ever lived.

But How About the Ones Who Play Today?

Okay, you want to know about Terry Bradshaw, Earl Campbell, Walter Payton, Billy Sims and the great teams like the Pittsburgh Steelers. Before we get into that, let's set the stage for them by pointing out the people who built the foundation for modern day football.

The first name that comes to mind is that of Paul Brown, the man who built the Cleveland Browns' dynasty. It was he who defined the potential of a great pass attack and great pass defense. He had a young quarterback named Otto Graham. About the best way to explain how good he was is to recount a story told by George Ratterman, a former member of the Buffalo Bills, and one of the better quarterbacks in the All-American Conference. When that conference was absorbed by the National Football League, Ratterman wound up with the Cleveland Browns—as a benchwarmer. When he was asked how it was possible that as talented a quarterback as himself rarely got into a game, the cherubic–faced athelete never hesitated, "Because Otto Graham is so much better than I am," he said. It was as simple as that. That's how good Otto Graham was. As Paul Brown put it: "He was a winner."

The same could be said of Bart Starr. He was the key that Vince Lombardi used to unlock the door to football immortality. Let's first talk about Lombardi. Some know him only as a coach, but he was a very fine college football player at Fordham University. He was later an assistant coach at West Point under Earl ("Red") Blaik, one of the finest coaches ever.

When Lombardi came to Green Bay, he was already experienced in coaching the pros, having been with the New York Giants. He then put all of his knowledge and talent into molding Bart Starr, just out of the University of Alabama, to be a star. Now there have been many outstanding quarterbacks in pro football—Sammy Baugh, Sid Luckman, Norm Van Brocklin and Bob Waterfield, just to name a few. Starr may not have been as technically great as some of them, but, like Otto Graham he had that one great quality—he was a winner. Really, when you think about the man—the one man—who deserves the title "the best" it would probably be Johnny Unitas. It's strange—here is a man who had been cut from the Pittsburgh Steelers and was actually ready to quit the game. Then, he got a call from the Baltimore Colts. Weeb Ewbanks, the same man who later coached Joe Namath, was at Baltimore when Johnny "U" showed. Two years later, the Colts were the champions of the pro football world. The 1958 meeting of the Baltimore Colts and the New York Giants has been called the greatest football game of all time. More than that, its impact on television was enormous. That game probably did more for football on television than anyone can imagine.

It was a dark, chilly day in New York, the way it always is in New York that time of year. These two great teams went at each other like a couple of prehistoric monsters. Now it was the fourth quarter. The lights in the stadium were on, and it looked really weird. Gino Marchetti, one of the best defensive ends the game had ever known, had just fractured his ankle stopping Frank Gifford inches short of a first down, and so the Giants had to kick. Now it was Baltimore's ball with less than two minutes to go, and the Giants leading, 17-14. The Colts were 86 yards from pay dirt.

The first two passes by Unitas were incomplete, so Johnny did the unexpected. He ran Lenny Moore for 11 yards and a first down. Johnny "U" threw and the great Raymond Berry caught. It was now first down on the 50 yard line. The Colts called time out with 64 seconds remaining. Twice more Unitas threw to Berry, with the clock running and no more time outs left, and with the ball on the Giants 13, Steve Myrha kicked a field goal and it was overtime.

The Giants won the toss and elected to receive, but they could not move the ball. When they kicked it was Baltimore's ball on the Colts' 20. Make way for Johnny. He moved his team in fitful spurts. Twice on big third down plays, he threw swing passes to his fullback. Allan Ameche, and the big guy just squeezed past the first down mark. Unitas then showed remarkable calm in the face of a Giant pass rush, and hit Raymond Berry of the Giant's 44. Here, Unitas displayed field generalship by faking a pass and giving the ball to Allan Ameche; the battering ram took it 24 yards further. The Colts kept it going until Ameche banged into pay dirt—23-17 Baltimore. There had never been a better game.

No, New York fans, not even the day Joe Namath pulled off the impossible and led the New York Jets to their Super Bowl win over Baltimore. "Broadway Joe" was cast in the mold of Johnny Unitas, but injuries robbed him of an even greater career than he had.

Which brings us to Terry Bradshaw, "Mean Joe" Greene, and the other greats who have made the Pittsburgh Steelers into what many feel is the greatest football team ever. From 1975 to 1980, The Steelers won four Super Bowls. They beat Minnesota in 1975, 16-6, they beat Dallas in 1976, 21-17. They repeated themselves, and again beat Dallas in 1979, 35-31, and Los Angeles in 1980, 31-19. You realize, of course, that no other team has even won three Super Bowl championships.

While the record book will show that Franco Harris is the leading rusher in Super Bowl history, and that Lynn Swann is the leading pass catcher; that John Stallworth, Jack Lambert, Jack Ham, Joe Greene, Dwight White, and countless others have contributed greatly—there is no question that Terry

Bradshaw was the heart of his team. Like Bart Starr, Otto Graham, and John Unitas, Bradshaw is able to exact victories where defeat seems inevitable.

We've mentioned Earl Campbell. He's the closest thing to Jimmy Brown ever. Like Brown, he has great size, great mobility and surprising speed. Will he ever wipe out Brown's records? Only time will tell. As for Walter Payton, his name ranks high on the list that began one day when a man named Beattie Feathers, playing for the Chicago Bears in 1934, became the first to rush for a thousand yards in a season. Like Feathers, Billy Sims rushed

The Man with the Golden Arm—Joe Namath

A bundle of TNT—Earl Campbell

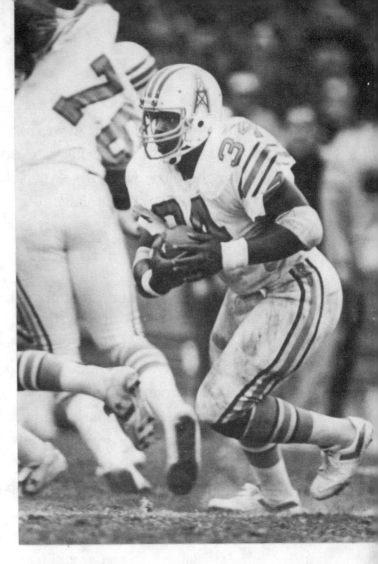

for over a thousand yards in his first professional year. Unlike Feathers, Sims will do it many more times.

"They are getting bigger, faster, and stronger" is a statement you hear a great deal these days. It is obviously true. But size is not the decisive factor in making a great runner. They come in all sizes and shapes. They do all have one thing in common, though; they hate to be tackled.

The reason I mention that is that while sitting here and writing about players who have made their marks playing in the National Football League, I am suddenly struck by the enormous disparity in their sizes, shapes, and styles. One thinks of the enormous elegance of a George McAffee, and Ollie Matson, or that of a Gayle Sayers. The illusiveness of Hugh McElhenny, and Buddy Young. Then there is the brute power of Bronko Nagurski, Jimmy Brown, Earl Campbell and Jim Taylor. Which style do you prefer? Because if you're young and a dreamer and worried about your size and shape—forget it. Just hate to be tackled.

Where and When Was the First Pro Football Game Played?

The town of Latrobe, Pennsylvania, about forty miles from Pittsburgh, earns the honor as the site of the first acknowledged pro game. Sponsored by the local Y.M.C.A., the game matched Latrobe against a team from the nearby town of Jeannette. It was played on August 31, 1895. The home team won, 12-0, and the players were paid ten dollars each.

For the next twenty-five years the sport was concentrated mainly in Pennsylvania, Ohio, Indiana, Illinois and New York. Teams were casually organized, scheduling was an impromptu affair, and the better players shifted to wherever the money beckoned. The pay was low, with few getting more than a hundred dollars per game. Many collegians played under pseudonyms on Sundays, after their Saturday varsity efforts. Knute Rockne, after he was graduated from Notre Dame, was supposed to have set some sort of record by playing for six different teams in one season.

That same year, Connie Mack organized his baseball athletics into a football team and claimed the world championship after his club defeated Pittsburgh, 12-6. Pittsburgh had a fullback named Christy Mathewson who had been a football standout at Bucknell and had just started his magnificent baseball career. Heated rivalries sprang up among such Ohio towns as Canton, Akron, Massillon, Columbus and Dayton. The great Jim Thorpe began his pro career with Canton in 1915 and was a terror for the next decade. He had an interesting custom of covering his shoulder pads with sheet metal, which made tackling him a memorable experience. By 1920, the time was thought to be at hand to try to organize the first pro football league. Named the American Professional Football Association, it was the forerunner of the National Football League. Eleven teams joined and the fee was a flat $100. The teams were the Akron Professionals, the Dayton Triangles, the Cleveland Indians, the Canton Bulldogs, the Massillon Tigers, Rochester (N.Y.), Rock Island (Illinois), Muncie (Indiana), the Chicago Cardinals, and the Decatur (Illinois) Staleys. The meeting took place in the office of Ralph Hays, an auto dealer in Canton, on September 17, 1920. For the value of his name, Thorpe was elected president. However, by April of the next year, the league had to be reorganized, and Joe Carr, a former sports writer and manager of a Columbus team, took over as president, a position he held with distinction until he died in 1939.

Which Two Teams Played the Longest Pro Championship Game?

The Dallas Texans and the Houston Oilers in the 1962 A.F.L. title game. After the Texans ran up a 17-0 lead the first two quarters, the Oilers, with veteran George Blanda at the helm, came back in the second half and evened the score, Blanda converting after Charlie Tolar's one-yard buck early in the final period.

When the quarter ended in a 17-17 deadlock, halfback Abner Haynes, the Dallas offensive captain, went to mid-field for the coin toss. Haynes was instructed by Coach Hank Stram to pick the end of the field with the wind advantage. Haynes won the toss, but surprisingly said, "We'll kick." So Dallas lost both the advantage of receiving and the wind.

The unintended edge did not help the Oilers to score and the Texans were similarly frustrated through the first 15-minute overtime period, but they had the ball as the period ended.

At the beginning of the second extra period, Len Dawson completed a 10-yard pass to halfback Jack Spikes and Spikes raced for 19 yards to the Houston 19. Rookie Tommy Brooker became the Dallas hero of the day by kicking a 25-yard field goal at 2:58 and the Texans won, 20-17.

James A. Naismith (1861–1939)

BASKETBALL

There are no doubts as to who invented basketball and where. During the summer of 1890, the need for some new game became imperative at Springfield College (known then as the International Y.M.C.A. Training School) in Springfield, Massachusetts. Young coaches and athletic directors had gathered there from many different states for the summer term and all expressed complaints about the lack of interest in their winter gymnasium classes. There was little interest in the type of activity introduced by R. J. Roberts, a one-time circus performer who had inaugurated a system of exercises that he termed body-building work.

The directors of the school agreed that what was needed was an indoor team sport that could compete successfully with football and baseball, which were largely responsible for the Y.M.C.A.'s high summer and fall recruitment of members.

They turned the whole problem over to Dr. James A. Naismith, a Canadian instructor at the school, and they couldn't have picked a better man. Dr. Naismith was the type who went about things methodically. He first examined all outdoor-team sports, and noticed that what most of them had in common was that they used a ball which was driven, thrown, or struck toward a goal. All right, he'd start with a ball, but since the game he was seeking would have to be played indoors, it could not be small and hard like a baseball. An uncontrolled baseball would be dangerous.

Second, he took note that the most popular team sports featured body contact and hard running, both of which would be hazardous in a small area with hard floors. His game would have to be slowed down somehow, with no hard rampant running and embodying a minimum of body contact. Along with this he noticed that the roughest play occurred when one team was near another's goal.

His solutions to these problems? First, use a large, lightweight ball, like a soccer ball, which could be easily controlled and wouldn't damage the players or the premises if it did get out of control. Second, make it illegal to run with the ball (have the man in possession bounce it along, or something like that) or to gain possession by wrestling it from an opponent by brute force. As for rough play around the goals, eliminate it by placing the goals over the players' heads. (Who could get hurt jumping up and down under a goal?)

Sometime during the winter of 1890–1891, Dr. Naismith nailed up two peach baskets at opposite ends of the gymnasium, chose up sides, threw in a soccer ball, and basketball was born!

How Did the Dribble Come into Being?

The dribble was originally a defensive measure. When a player had possession of the ball and was so closely guarded that he could not pass it to one of his teammates, the only thing he could do was to lose possession

Dr. James A. Naismith, surrounded by players of the first basketball team.

voluntarily in such a way that he might possibly recover it. He accomplished this by rolling or bouncing the ball on the floor. In a short time, players realized that by bouncing the ball rapidly they could control it as well.

During the Christmas vacation of 1891 some of the Springfield College students went home and began playing the game in their own local Y.M.C.A.'s. There were no rules in print at the time, so each student had his own particular version of the game.

It wasn't until January, 1892, that the rules of the game were published (in the school paper) under the heading, "A New Game."

The first set of printed rules signalled the rapid spread of basketball to all parts of the United States, Europe and South America. Soldiers introduced basketball in the Philippines in 1900, and the U.S. army of occupation taught the game to the Germans during World War I.

However, it wasn't until 1936 that basketball got its biggest boost when it was included in the Olympic Games at Berlin. Basketball had finally arrived as a major sport.

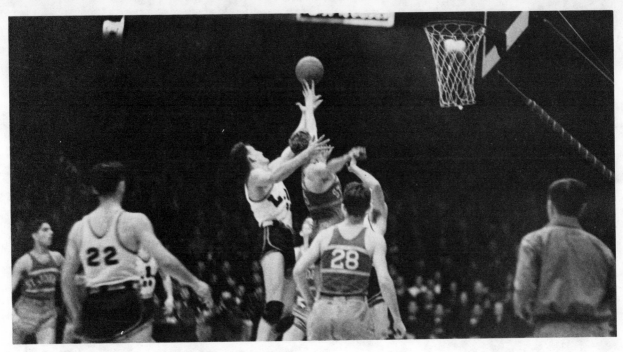

An early college basketball game in Madison Square Garden.

From then on, basketball—scholastic, collegiate and professional—grew even quicker than Topsy of *Uncle Tom's Cabin*.

One of the biggest boons to basketball's popularity was the staging of well-attended double-headers at New York City's Madison Square Garden. These games, more than any one thing, placed basketball in the big time. In addition, the intersectional games played at the Garden were of paramount importance in standardizing rule interpretations and introducing all styles of play of all parts of the nation.

The start of college basketball at Madison Square Garden was on December 29, 1934. Ask any basketball fan which teams played in that opening double-header and they will always recall two of them.

What is the Record for Consecutive NCAA Championships?

Back in the days before the "Wizard of Westwood", the great John Wooden, began the "golden era" at UCLA, no college had ever won more than two championships in a row. But Mr. Wooden took care of that. Beginning in 1967, UCLA won seven championships in a row. To say this feat is incredible is the understatement of all understatements in sports.

Actually, during the period from 1954 to 1975, the U clans won the championship ten times. That skein was interrupted by Texas El Paso in 1966 and by North Carolina State in 1974.

There can be no overlooking the fact that such great players as Lew Alcindor (Kareem Abdul Jabbar), Gail Goodrich, Bill Walton, and Sidney Wicks, as the men on the floor were the producers of the victories that went into the making of championships. But—and make no mistake about this—the catalytic agent was John Wooden. It was he who brought these people to UCLA and it was he who molded them into the force they became. There may never be another "Golden Era" like it again.

Mind you there have been other great coaches. Hank Iba took his Oklahoma A & M team to back-to-back crowns in 1945 and 1946. The first time any college had achieved such success. Coach Iba had a great basketball player named Bob Kurland—and it was with this young giant that Iba fashioned the first back-to-backer. He never was able to do it as well again. And he was a great coach.

So was the Baron from Kentucky—Adolph Rupp. With such great players as Ralph Beard and Alex Groza, the Wildcats put together two championships in 1948 and 1949. Although they were to win again, they never produced another back-to-backer.

It was another six years before the University of San Francisco performed the feat. Coach Phil Woolpert had the legendary Bill Russell and a collection of outstanding supporting players. But it was two and no more.

Five years later, in 1961, Coach Ed Jucker, without a single super star, brought the University of Cincinnati into the exclusive back-to-back club. It stopped at two.

I would be remiss not to mention Nat Holman. This legendary basketball star of the original Celtics—a man ranked an all time great player—was the coach of the City College of New York in 1950. That year the Beavers produced a twin win that will never be repeated. They won both the NCAA and the NIT. Since no team can compete in both tournaments now, it obviously will never happen again.

Who Was Basketball's First Big Man?

George Mikan, 6 feet 10 inches, 250 pounds, was the first of the truly great big men. His is an unusual story, in that Mikan was not much of a high school ball player. He tried getting into Notre Dame, but wasn't considered good enough to make it, so he turned to DePaul University, coached by a former Notre Dame star, Ray Meyers, and gained stardom. Meyers worked extended hours with Mikan and the combination of both their desires and energy produced a "superstar." And Mikan was just that. He was a college All-American in 1944, 1945 and 1946. Then he went on to professional basketball and completely dominated the sport. He was the reason that the Minneapolis Lakers (now the Los Angeles Lakers) were the kingpins. He spent ten years with the Lakers and was the first player to reach the 10,000-point scoring plateau. In Mikan's first seven seasons with the Lakers, Minneapolis won six championships. George was no graceful gazelle on the court. He was more like a stampeding elephant, dominating the backboards by sheer brute strength and power.

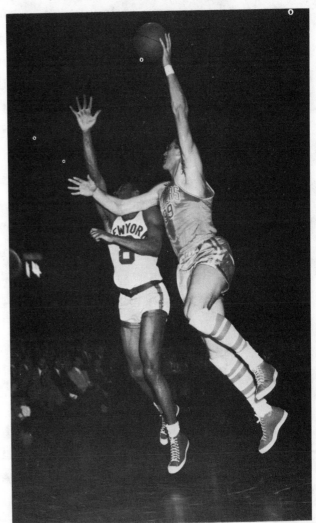

George Mikan hooking a shot in against Nat ("Sweetwater") Clifton of the New York Knicks.

When it came time to pick the greatest player of the half-century, Mikan was the choice. He is the perfect example of what determination and desire can do. Of course, being 6 feet 10 inches tall and weighing 250 pounds doesn't hurt, either.

Who Influenced Defense More Than Any Other Player?

The answer here is Bill Russell. More than any one player, he dominated the sport by his superb defense. It's amazing that Big Bill would have to settle for being just an ordinary offensive ball player. But on defense he is a genius. There simply has never been a player of his size with his mobility, and quickness and anticipation. He would actually change the other team's offense. For one thing, any time a player from the opposition got past the backcourt men or the forwards and went driving for the hoop, there was Russell. That wasn't the end of it. If you passed off to a teammate, Russell could recover and switch to the man who had just been handed the ball. He terrorized players into changing the arc of their shots. And he gave his teammates the added capability of playing their men closer because they weren't afraid that the man might drive around them. If he did, Russell was always waiting. Since he came into the N.B.A. in 1956, Russell and his Boston Celtics have lost the N.B.A. championship only twice. In 1958, the St. Louis Hawks—with Bob Pettit, Clyde Lovellette and Cliff Hagan—beat Boston, but it should be pointed out that Russell was ill and out of several games. In 1967, "Wilt the Stilt" and the Philadelphia team tripped up the Celts. Other than that, the Boston entry has ruled the roost like no team in no other sport. And when he's asked why, the answer from Bill Russell is always the same: "You win with defense." You sure do, when that defense is someone named Bill Russell.

Who is "Wilt the Stilt"?

Every sport has one man about whom controversies wax hot and heavy. In basketball, it's Wilt Chamberlain. The reason is obvious, if you've ever seen Wilt. And how could you miss? At seven feet one inch and somewhere around 290 pounds, he's easily the strongest big man the game has ever known. If Mikan was like a stampeding elephant, then Wilt was like a herd of them, when the spirit moved him. The easiest way to get Wilt upset was to suggest that the spirit didn't always move him. Wilt, though, would have the kind of nights no one in the history of the sport could approach. There was, for example, a night in Hershey, Pennsylvania, when the Big Dipper decided to pour it on, and scored one hundred points against the New York Knicks. It's the record, of course, and even though it was set against a team that wasn't one of the strongest, bear in mind that Wilt holds the scoring record in every arena in the league. He didn't just pick the easy ones.

His battles with Bill Russell are legends. That Russell could even give him a tussle is really a testimonial to Russell's tremendous winning desire. It's no secret that prior to some important games Russell has become sick to his stomach from anxiety. That's how intense a competitor he is.

No one knows for sure that Chamberlain doesn't get that intense, too. The fact is, he has always been so much stronger, faster, and taller than almost everyone he has played against. Maybe he resented the fact that fans expected so much more from him. Then, too, there was always the embarrassment of the way he shot fouls. He just couldn't shoot fouls well, no matter what style he used. One-hand, two-hand, overhand, underhand, sidearm. Here was the basket, just fifteen feet away, with no one in the way, and all you had to do was put the ball in. Wilt couldn't. He's probably the only player ever with a better percentage from the field than the foul line.

And his life story has been a repeat story. He went to Kansas and everyone predicted that Kansas would win three championships. They didn't win even one. Well, you could excuse that by saying that he didn't have a good enough supporting cast. But the story

Bill Russell, player-coach of the Boston Celtics, brings his defensive prowess into play by blocking a shot by Keith Erickson of the Los Angeles Lakers in the final game of the 1969 N.B.A. championship play-offs. The Celtics went on to win another title.

was the same when he got to the pros. Added to his torment was his apparent inability to communicate with his coaches. They added to the engima of a Gulliver-like tale. With all that height, all that speed, all that jumping ability, and all that incredible strength, how could he be tied down? It remains a mystery.

Who is the Best All-Around Player?

Even old-timers agree that the "Big O", Oscar Robertson, merits this distinction. His size and his skill are unmatched. Even though players today are bigger than ever, faster than ever, shoot better and jump better, no one player combines the talents Oscar had.

Certainly, the great Dr. J, Julius Erving, is more exciting. There never has been a player as elegant and ballet-like in his movements as this man. And there are those who suggest that George Gervin, Peter Marovich and Walt Frazier had incredible skills. But there was only one "Big O". Oscar was a genius on offense. Even if he didn't score a point he could run a team like a coach. As a matter of fact, some players thought him a dictator. I suppose the only player who really could compare to Oscar was Jerry West. Although Jerry was smaller than Robertson, his skills on offense and defense were almost on a par except in one area. Jerry West was not a play-maker. Jerry was at his best as a shooting guard. I don't intend to detract from his greatness. Jerry West belongs on the same plateau as Bill Russell, Wilt Chamberlain, and Elgin Baylor. But when they pass out the slips that are marked—who is the best—the answer here is Oscar Robertson.

Versatile Oscar Robertson dribbles his way through the Boston Celtics toward the basket.

What is the Greatest Scoring Combination in the History of Pro Basketball?

Jerry West and Elgin Baylor of the Los Angeles Lakers. Jerry West is a coach's dream. From the time he made his debut on the national scene while with the West Virginia Mountaineers, West has been a prime example of the All-American boy—modest, retiring, never a harsh word about anyone, and always putting out on the basketball court. No one could shoot it any better than Jerry. He's only a shade over six feet two, but he's really got spring in his legs. He can get up so high so quick that it's impossible to block his shot and he really goes to the hoop. No matter whether it's Bill Russell, or whoever, under that basket, West will go for the hoop, and most of the time it's good for two. In addition, West will give it everything he's got on defense. When West plays you, you've got to earn your points. If there was one phase of the game that wasn't quite up to the rest, it's the fact that Jerry's not a playmaker.

His teammate with the Lakers, Elgin Baylor, is probably the greatest offensive six-foot-five player in the history of the game. Baylor's body control is unmatched in basketball play. Watching him go up in the air and hang, or float, or just do anything, is worth the price of admission. Baylor learned the game in Washington, D.C. As a youngster, he used to practice by himself and he perfected all those incredible moves. Elgin comes to a man dribbling the ball, and then turns his back to the hoop, maneuvering, weaving and bobbing. Then, with that incredible "step" toward the basket, *bingo!* he scores two more.

Baylor originally was at the College of Idaho, but switched to Seattle University. There he turned the Chieftains into a power. You may not remember, though, that when Baylor came east to play in the N.I.T. he was not exactly sensational. Seattle played against St. Bonaventure, and the Brown Indians from Olean used a tactic that stunned the crowd. Instead of using one of their bigger players to guard Baylor, they gave the task to a six-foot-one guard named Brendan McCann, and it worked. St. Bona upset Baylor and Seattle. After the game there were many in the crowd at Madison Square Garden who talked about how overrated Baylor was.

His first in the N.B.A. stopped all that talk. He wasn't good, or great. He was superstar material. Elgin averaged 34.9 points per game and despite being a small forward at 6′5″, he hauled down 1.050 rebounds. The Lakers jumped from last to second and beat St. Louis for the division title. It took the Boston Celtics to stop them.

Elgin Baylor of the Los Angeles Lakers jumps up to score against the St. Louis Hawks.

Jerry West of the Los Angeles Lakers.

Which Player Started the Basketball Scoring Revolution?

Angelo Enrico (Hank) Luisetti, born January 16, 1916 in the Telegraph Hill section of San Francisco, the same area which provided the New York Yankees with Joe DiMaggio, Frank Crosetti and Tony Lazzeri, is credited with giving basketball the same prominence Babe Ruth gave baseball and Red Grange, football. Before Luisetti came along, the game was a two-handed game. Occasionally someone would heave the ball at the basket with just one hand, but the instance was so rare and it brought forth such a quick "Cut that out!" from the coach that no one did it. Then Luisetti came east to Madison Square Garden to play against the best and to prove his claim to stardom. It was easy. Luisetti made the one-handed shot famous and basketball has never been the same since. Hank was tremendous at the Garden, but it was only the beginning. He moved on to Pittsburgh against a first-rate Duquesne team where he scored fifty points. That year he scored 305 points in eighteen games. It may not seem much by today's standards, but in those days it was the best.

There was only one other thing to add to the scoring punch. That last addition was the jump shot. There have been a lot of opinions on who originated the shot, but most people allow that it was Kenny Sailors, one-time Wyoming University star and later a stand-out in the pros, who brought it into prominence. There are some who insist that John "Bud" Palmer, New York City's official greeter under Mayor John Lindsay, was one of the originals while playing for the New York Knickerbockers. One thing is certain, though, with the jump shot, the offensive player has had an advantage his predecessors never knew.

Hank Luisetti, of Stanford University, the greatest basketball player of his time.

Who Were the Original Celtics?

This was a group of players which started as a semi-pro team in 1915. The Celtics dominated the American Basketball League formed in 1925 and one season won 109 out of 120 games. They were then thrown out of the league for being too strong. The Celtics put the show on the road and became bywords throughout the country. They would play about 150 games a year, winning 90 percent of them. At Cleveland, in 1922, they played before 23,000 spectators. The outstanding players on the Celtics included Joe Lapchick, Ernie Reich, Johnnie Beckman, Pete Barry, Chris Leonard, Dave Banks, George Haggerty, Elmer Ripley, Harry Brugge, Benny Borgman, "Stretch" Meehan, "Chief" Mueller, Jim Kane and two men who had enormous impact on the game, Nat Holman and "Dutch" Dehnert. It was Dehnert who was given credit for starting the "pivot" play in basketball. All he did was turn his back to the basket and set screens.

As for Holman, this incredible human was without peer in his own day as a ball player. He could run, pass and dribble superbly. His two-handed set shot was deadly. Nat went on after his playing days to become one of the great coaches of all time. It was his City College team of 1950 which won the NCAA and NIT in the same year. That hadn't ever happened before and probably won't again unless the rules are changed to allow a team to play in both tournaments. There is no relationship between the original Celtics and the Boston Celtics.

Who Started the Harlem Globetrotters?

Abe Saperstein, a little man with a big dream, was the creator of the Harlem Globetrotters. It all started back in 1927 when Saperstein combined five players and an old automobile and started on the road.

The story of the Globetrotters has been told in a movie version, but the movies couldn't capture the whole flavor of it. Touring over millions of miles, the Globetrotters have been the greatest basketball ambassadors the game has ever known. Just name a place, whether it be Juneau, Alaska, or some spot in the arid area of the world, and they have been there. They have traveled by car, plane, ship, boat, horse and wagon—even by dogsled—and wherever they have played, they have delighted capacity crowds. They may not rank as one of the great playing teams, but their showmanship is incomparable. They have one purpose and one purpose only—to entertain the crowds. Who can forget Reece (Goose) Tatum, the man they called the Clown Prince of Basketball? With an arm span of 84 inches, the fact that he was only six feet three inches tall became meaningless. Goose did for children what Walt Disney did. He ran the gamut of their emotions and they loved him. Another outstanding player was Marques Haynes, a spectacular dribbler. Marques did everything with a basketball but eat it. When he dribbled the ball while on his knees with a speed and dexterity no one else

could ever display, the crowd would "ooh" and "aah." Other key men included Ermer Robinson, Clarence Wilson, Josh Grider, William "Rookey" Brown and Sam Wheeler. These were the Harlem Globetrotters. And they're still going strong.

Reece ("Goose") Tatum of Harlem Globetrotters, putting on one of his typical clowning acts.

Which Team Holds the Longest Scholastic Winning Streak?

Coach Ernie Blood's Passaic (N.J.) wonder team ran up 159 consecutive victories before losing to Hackensack (N.J.), 39-35, on February 6, 1925. More recently, Power Memorial High School, with Lew Alcindor, ran off 71 straight before they ran into De Matha High School of Hyattsville, Maryland, which stopped the Power streak.

What is Meant by a Combination Man-For-Man Zone?

This is about as good a time as any to go into defenses in basketball. There are differences in the pros where you cannot play a zone, although some of the teams hedge a little. But in amateur ball, you're allowed to use any defense. A man-for-man defense can be defined as one in which each defensive player is assigned a particular opponent, and during the rest of the game he sticks with him, no matter what. They tell the story of some players who would guard their assigned opponent from the time he came out of the dressing room.

Now, when a zone defense is in use, each player is stationed in a certain terrortory on the floor and is only responsible for the player in his territory or zone. In its simplest form, that's the difference between the man-for-man and the zone defense.

But there are too many in the business with enormous imagination for the game to have such simplistic form. At Notre Dame, one such man was the late great George Keogan. Recognizing the difficulties involved in straight man-for-man guarding, Coach Keogan used a "switching man-for-man."

Later, Eddie Hickey, while coaching at St. Louis University with enormous success, added his own variations to the "switching" so that teams not only used lateral switches but also vertical. The result was that you couldn't tell the difference between Coach Hickey's defense and the zone defense. To add to the confusion, there were coaches like Joe Mullaney at Providence and Jack Kraft at Villanova who would combine and play you man-for-man on one side and zone on the other. This type of maneuvering was called a "Chinese" defense. It added to the woes of many teams. When watching a game, here's a way to determine what kind of defense a team is using. If a player on the offense runs toward the basket without the ball and is followed by one man, you can be pretty sure it's a man-for-man. Now, I admit that that makes it seem a little simpler than it sometimes is, but that's really the basis of it all. Today, most coaches will use that principle right at the start of a play. They'll just run a man through without the ball. If no one picks him up all the way, then they'll go into the zone offense.

What is the All-Court Press?

Actually, it's just what it sounds like. The defensive team picks you up from the time you take the ball out of bounds. Some teams used this strategy to slow you down in back-court while they set up a zone defense. Other teams use it to force you into a running game. That's the technique U.C.L.A. used so well against a bigger, stronger Michigan team that was also slower. When they got the Wolverines to run with them, they destroyed them. There's the man-for-man all-court press and the zone all-court press. The idea is the same as for the man-for-man and one that's played half-court. Just apply the same principles to full court and you've got it.

What are Offensive Formations?

Against a man-for-man defense, the standard is that if you've got a real big man, you get him as close to the basket as possible and let him put the ball in. This is where you hear the term "pivot man." That's the player with his back

65

to the loop who keeps edging in close to the basket. If a team doesn't have that big man, you'll hear them say, "Keep the middle open." That simply means, "Give the smaller players a chance to use their speed and drive to go down the unclogged middle."

Once you get into operating against a zone, the formations are as many and varied as you can imagine. There's the three-two, the two-three, the two-one-two, the one-three-one, and the three-one-one.

Obviously, it's impossible to capture the entire scope of basketball in just a few pages, but with these fundamentals, your idea of the game should be somewhat broader. The rest is up to you. Playing and viewing and reading extensively about the game will eventually get you your Ph.D.

3-2 zone defense

2-3 zone defense

2-1-2 zone defense

1-3-1 zone defense

2-2-1 zone defense

3-1-1 zone defense

James J. Jeffries and Bob
Fitzsimmons in the ring.

BOXING

There is nothing that can arouse greater passions in men than boxing.
You can get into a heated argument just by bringing up the subject and
stating whether or not it should be abolished. Try it sometime. Just say to
someone, "Boxing ought to be abolished." Get ready for a real argument. That's the nature of the "sport."

It has probably been that way since some ancient time when two men
first got into a discussion that they couldn't settle with their mouths.
"Oh, you think I'm wrong? . . . Well, put up your fists!"

You might suppose that because the word "pugilism" is derived from
the Latin *pugil* (one who fights with his fists) it all began in ancient Rome.
But Dr. E. A. Speiser and some of his associates have discovered slabs
and figurines in a temple near Baghdad in Mesopotamia depicting men
fighting with their fists prior to the time of the Romans and Greeks.

67

However, the Greeks really exploited boxing on a level that was unknown before them. When the Romans conquered Greece, they added their own refinements.

Boxing as we know it today has its roots in England (like baseball and football). The first recorded bouts took place over 250 years ago. James Figg is listed as the originator of bare-knuckle fighting. Figg was an excellent all-around athlete and he brought a new style to bare-knuckle fighting. Instead of wasting time trying to wrestle his opponents, as was the custom, he'd get in as close as he could, and when the other man tried to grab him, he'd just sock it to him. Since his opponents knew nothing about defense, Figg would have little trouble belting them. He either knocked them out or made them helpless.

He was an instant hit. Everyone talked about "Figg's Fighting." Figg became a teacher of the art of hitting a man on the chin. He retired as the undefeated champion. When he died, it was due to pneumonia.

After Figg's death, the next important figure in the sport was Jack Broughton. Broughton was considered (by the standards of his time) a great student of the sport. A public outcry to lessen the brutality of the sport prompted Broughton to draw up a set of fixed rules. He introduced them at a bout that took place on August 10, 1743.

While Figg ruled the roost, men had to continue fighting until there was a definite winner or loser; no rest periods were allowed. Broughton changed all that. His rules became known as the Broughton rules, and they governed boxing for many years. Then came the Marquis of Queensberry rules which were intended to keep boxing from being barbarous. There is still some question, even today, as to whether the Marquis succeeded. Much depends on the individual boxing fan. There are some who still "scream for blood," when they think the fighting is too tame.

In the early days in America, boxing was not viewed with favor. The first American champion was a gent named Jacob Hyer. All he had to do to win the crown was beat a man in a grudge fight—there was no one else really interested in challenging him. Twenty-four years later his son Tom announced that he had succeeded his father as champion. That was that.

But news gets around fast, even when something is not viewed with favor. Some English fighters were soon battling here in the United States.

John L. Sullivan

Still, they drew only small crowds and made small news. Then along came a fighter named Paddy Ryan, who had had only four fights before meeting the English titleholder, Joe Goss. But Ryan beat Goss, and that made him world's champ. That still doesn't make it all sound too impressive. But then a fellow named John L. Sullivan appeared on the scene, and boxing now had its own Joe Namath. Sullivan was the man who brought boxing into focus. It got to the point where people were walking around saying, "Shake the hand that shook the hand of John L." That's how big John L. Sullivan was, and this was in a time even before radio. John L. was smart enough to know that he had to give the sport some "show biz." When he did, the sport took off like a moon rocket.

James J. Corbett—"Gentleman Jim"

Who Beat John L. Sullivan?

The man was James J. Corbett. "Gentleman Jim," they called him when he came into fame. He was from San Francisco, and he was the first boxer to "hit the big time." Sullivan, who had brought boxing from bare knuckles to gloves, was still just a brawler compared to this San Francisco dandy. Corbett boxed his ears off before knocking him out in the twenty-first round. They fought for a purse of $25,000 and a side bet of $10,000. Like Sullivan, Corbett subsequently embarked on a stage career. He was the more serious actor and starred in "Gentleman Jack," "The Cadet," and "Cashel Byron's Profession."

It took a most unlikely looking gent to knock off Gentleman Jim. He was "Ruby Bob" Fitzsimmons. Fitzsimmons not only won the heavyweight crown, but before he hung up his gloves he also won the middleweight and light heavyweight crowns. (He and Henry Armstrong are the only two

70

fighters ever to win three different titles.) "Ruby Bob" was a string bean who could punch with unbelievable power. He fought until he was 52 years old (older even than Archie Moore). Fitzsimmons lost the heavyweight crown in his first defense of the title to one of the all-time great fighters, James J. Jeffries.

Who Was the "Manassa Mauler"?

The man who answered to that description was the one and only Jack Dempsey. So long as there is boxing there will always be arguments about who was the greatest fighter of all time—Was it Muhammed Ali,—Rocky Marciano,—Ray Robinson,—Benny Leonard,—Henry Armstrong,—Joe Gans,—or was it Jack Dempsey? Who knows? But one thing is certain. It was Jack Dempsey who brought boxing into the million dollar business that it has become. Like Ali, there was no place on the face of the globe where people didn't known Jack. Even today, an introduction of Dempsey will bring a crowd to a roar of acclaim. Strangely enough, after he all but killed Jess Willard to win the title on July 4, 1919, Dempsey was roundly criticized because he had seen no service in World War I. Despite the fact that he participated in some of the greatest fights of all time, Dempsey's image was always somewhat tarnished. But all that changed when he fought Gene Tunney. Dempsey was beaten and as so often happens when a man loses, he regained popular sentiment. Then, if he hadn't regained it all, there was the return fight with Gene Tunney and the "long count" incident which made him the most popular sports figure in the country. Now please remember that this was the time of Babe Ruth, "Red" Grange, Bobby Jones, Bill Tilden, and the others whose contributions served to make this an era they called "golden". But everyone felt that Dempsey had gotten a raw deal from the referee who had allowed more than ten seconds to elapse before sending the two men to fight. Dempsey had charisma—now he had love. His style of fighting—mauling—made him a natural. He came to fight, to be hit and to hit back, and that's all a fighter really needs.

Jack Dempsey, the
"Manassa Mauler,"
in training.

Which Fighter Scored the Most One-Round Knockouts in Title Fights?

Joe Louis was the most destructive exponent of the one-round knockout in title bouts. Louis scored ten of them in his career and five of these came in bouts with his title at stake. His quickest and most brutal was inflicted in 2 minutes 4 seconds the night he *blitzkrieged* Max Schmeling, an emissary out of Hitler's Germany who had gotten a telegram from the *Fuehrer* before the fight asking him to uphold the honor of the Master Race. It had to be the most satisfying experience of Louis' career. This fine young man, who had battled his way from the amateurs to the big time and had taken the world of boxing by storm with his ability and gentlemanly demeanor, had been badly battered in his first meeting with Schmeling. He had been knocked out in twelve rounds after taking a terrible beating. But getting knocked out in the ring was the least of it. Schmeling not only put him down in the ring but he "put him down" out of it. He belittled Louis both as a fighter and a man. The result was that the "Brown Bomber," as Louis was known, ached to get back at him, and when he finally got his chance, he more than evened the score.

How Many Heavyweight Champions Retired Undefeated?

Technically, only four—James J. Jeffries, Gene Tunney, Joe Louis and Rocky Marciano. (Muhammad Ali did not retire.) Jeffries and Louis both attempted comebacks and were unsuccessful. Gene Tunney is probably the most underrated fighter of all time. This ex-marine never captured the public fancy for a number of reasons. First of all, he read poetry, and that didn't sit too well with the fight public. And secondly, he beat Jack Dempsey. It made a hero of Dempsey and made Tunney even less popular.

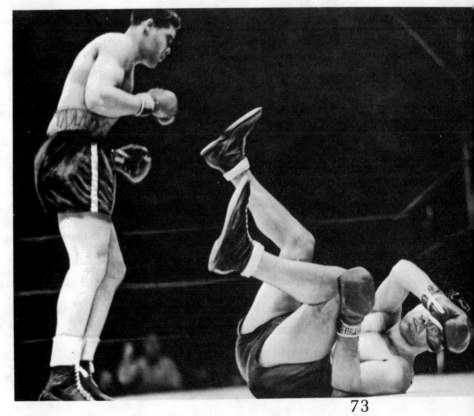

After losing to Max Schmeling in a previous bout, Joe Louis turned the tables in their second match, producing one of the quickest finishes to a world-heavyweight fight.

Harry Greb

Gene Tunney taking the much-disputed "long count" in the famous title fight with Jack Dempsey.

Actually, Gene was everything you'd want in a fighter. He could box, punch, and he had tremendous courage. His fights with Harry Greb are considered to be as viciously fought as any in the history of the game. Greb, in their first meeting, gave Tunney a fearful shellacking. A less courageous man would have quit the business. Gene not only didn't quit, but came back to beat Greb. When he hung up his gloves, Gene married into society—and that, along with the poetry, has made him seem outside the fold.

As for Rocky Marciano, they threw away the mold after they made him. He came out of Brockton, Massachusetts, and under the tutelage of Charlie Goldman, the 5′ 11″ 185-pounder blockbusted his way to the championship. Marciano was strictly a made fighter. He was not what the fight crowd would call a natural. He did it all through sheer courage and hard work. No fighter ever worked harder than Marciano, who actually enjoyed training. It was this superb conditioning that stood him in such good stead. He would come into the ring to fight and fight and fight. He'd hit you anywhere. In some of his fights he wore his opponents down by hitting them on the arms.

74

Then he'd shift his target to the head and that was all there was to it. Like Dempsey, Marciano is a soft-spoken man. But his fists spoke loud and clear. He was never beaten as a professional. Forty-nine fights, forty-nine wins—forty-three of them by knockout.

The unbeaten heavyweight champion, Rocky Marciano.

Where Does Muhammad Ali Fit In?

I guess you'd have to say he fits in anywhere. Ali was more than a prize fighter. He was a great athlete. I guess the fact that he was really as pretty as he said, tended to detract from the reality that in his prime at 6'3", 220 pounds, he was a hulk of a man. He also had great foot and hand speed. All the attributes to have made him into a great tight end in modern football. He could've played baseball or basketball. He chose instead to become a fighter. And what a fighter. Olympic Gold Medal Winner. Three time heavyweight champion. His defeat of the monstrous George Foreman. His "Thrilla in Manila" with Joe Frazier. It all reads like modern day legend. And you know, it is. Ali became bigger than life. A historical figure, a symbol to the world. This is no exaggeration. Muhammad Ali transcended his sport because the man represented more than the fighter. It's funny, that almost every fighter who attains greatness has detractors about his fistic ability. When Dempsey was champ they said Jack Johnson would have beaten him. When Joe Louis was champ they said Dempsey would've beaten him. When

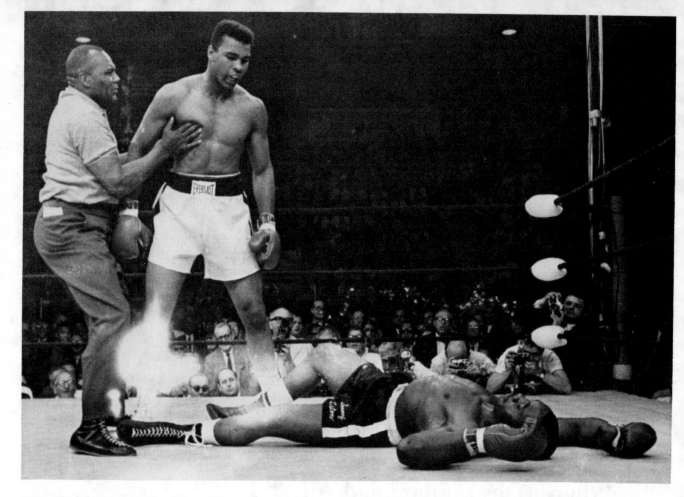

Muhammed Ali, then known as Cassius Clay, after knocking down Sonny Liston in their second title bout.

Marciano was champ they said he wasn't as good as Louis or Dempsey. With Ali, same story. I suppose he could be faulted on his lack of a great knockout punch. But every champion—every champion—was flawed. Let it be said of Ali that there never was one like him and there won't be another.

Who Were Outstanding in the Other Divisions?

Besides the heavyweight division, the two others that have provided the most memorable champions are the lightweight and the middleweight classes. In the lightweight division, the first really great one was a fighter named Joe Gans. He was born Joseph Gaines on November 25, 1874, in Baltimore. He started as a pro in 1891 and finally got his chance for the world championship in 1900 against Frank Erne. It turned into a disappointment as Gans asked to have the fight stopped in the twelfth round because of an injury. He was so good that he often fought outside of his own weight class. Once he fought the great welterweight champion, the original Joe Walcott, the "Barbados Demon," and the fight ended in a draw. He remained the lightweight champion for six years until he was knocked out by Battling Nelson in the seventeenth round on July 4, 1908. He lost again to Nelson and had one more fight before retiring in 1909. One year later, on August 10, 1910, he died of tuberculosis in Baltimore. In his almost twenty years in the ring, the record books credit him with fifty-five knockouts in 156 matches, of which he lost only eight.

And then there was Benny Leonard. Benny came out of the tough east side of New York, where one had to fight just to live. From 1917 to 1924 Benny dominated the lightweight division. That's not to say that he didn't have any tough fights. There was a night with Lew Tendler when Benny, after having been decked out on his feet, talked his way out of trouble. "Is that the hardest you can hit?" Benny wanted to know. He got out of the jam and went on to win. Benny had all the tools of the trade—a great jab that he would hook off of, a marvelous right, and with all of that he was a boxing master. There are those who say that he was the greatest lightweight who ever laced on a pair of gloves. When he died, he died in the ring, refereeing a fight.

After Benny came some really good ones, the kind who deserve mention, like Tony Canzoneri and Barney Ross. They were outstanding. Both Tony and Barney were title-holders in other divisions. Barney also deserves mention as a hero of World War II.

But if you're ranking the superstars, the next one has to be Hammerin' Henry Armstrong. Armstrong, with the torso of a middleweight and the legs of a featherweight, came out of the West and left a record equalled by few. Everyone knows that he was a triple-crown winner. The only other man ever to do that was Bob Fitzsimmons. But did you know that in addition to winning the featherweight, lightweight and welterweight championships, Armstrong almost won the middleweight title from Ceferino Garcia? He fought Garcia, the middleweight champ, to a draw, and that's about as close as you can come. Hammerin' Henry was a perpetual motion machine—

Henry Armstrong after he won his third world boxing title.

when he climbed into the ring he never stopped swinging. It sometimes looked as if he was trying to chase his opponent right out of the ring, and there were probably quite a few who wished that they had never gotten into the ring with him, once the bell rang.

They've run out of the Gans, Leonard and Armstrong molds. As a matter of fact, they don't make them like Tony Canzoneri or Barney Ross any more. What did you say? He sounds like an old-timer? O.K., then let's move to the middleweights. Can you think of some of the old-timers? How does the name Stanley Ketchell strike you? Remember how we talked about the great heavyweight, Jack Johnson? Would you believe that Stanley Ketchell not only fought Johnson but actually knocked him down? It was the last thing Ketchell did in that fight, because when Johnson got up, he knocked Ketchell out pronto. Ketchell was called the Michigan Assassin. He was a terrific hitter who began fighting when he was only sixteen years old. The string of knockouts that he piled up was so long it seems hard to believe. Finally, he got a crack at Mike (Twin) Sullivan for the middleweight crown—and the next thing you knew, Ketchell had knocked him out in one round. He kept going like that until Bill Papke stiffened him in twelve, but in a rematch Ketchell evened things up. There was one match, though, that Ketchell couldn't even up. A man named Walter Dipley shot him on October 15, 1910. It was fatal.

In discussing Gene Tunney, the name of Harry Greb came up. Whenever the ring fans talk of great fighters, that name always will. He was one of the greatest of them all. They nicknamed him "The Human Windmill" for an obvious reason—he was really tireless and fearless. He would fight anybody, including heavyweights. As a matter of fact, he wanted to fight Jack Dempsey, but the heavyweight champion said no, thank you. When you got Greb in the ring, it felt as if you were being towed under water. His fight with Mickey Walker is one they always mention when talk gets around to all-time fights. Their fight in the ring wasn't the end of it. They met on the street that same night and started all over again! It's a tribute to Mickey Walker's skill that he would take on Greb twice in one night.

You're probably wondering, "Is he ever going to mention Ray Robinson?" Well, the time has come. Let's start from the beginning. Ray Robinson's name is really Walker Smith. But no matter what you call him by name, when you talk about his fighting, you're talking about one of the greatest. Ring experts rate him the best pound-for-pound fighter of his time. He started as a lightweight, but the first title he won was the welterweight crown. Then he won the middleweight crown. Then he lost the middleweight crown. Then he won it. Then he lost it. Then he won it. In all, he won the

Sugar Ray Robinson regaining the middleweight crown against Carmen Basilia.

middleweight championship *five* different times, and that's a record, not only middleweights, but for all weights.

Ray almost became a triple-crown winner. He fought Joey Maxim for the light heavyweight championship and was leading by a tremendous point-margin when he suffered heat prostration and couldn't come out for the fourteenth round. He wasn't the only one affected by the heat that night. The referee also collapsed. They could substitute for the referee, but when Robinson collapsed, no substitution was allowed and so Ray Robinson did not become a triple-crown champion. It was one of the fistic things that Robinson did not achieve.

What About "Sugar Ray" Leonard?

I have already said enough about Ray Robinson to suggest that he never had an equal at his weight. Even if they call him "Sugar," logic dictates that Ray Leonard is not quite as sweet. But then, he doesn't have to be. He is a man of his time and as such, fulfills his role. And what is that role? The most charismatic fighter of his period. No, not like Ali. Television had not yet progressed sufficiently to make Ali even larger than he already is. Ray

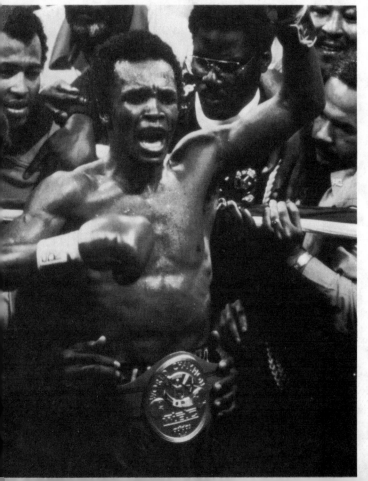

Leonard, although he doesn't like to hear it, is a television product. From that moment in Montreal when he won the Olympic Gold Medal, to those moments when he twice fought Roberto Duran, Leonard has been the most marketable prize fighter in history. His commercials attest to that. And if they didn't, just check out the amount of

The Man with The Midas Touch,
Sugar Ray Leonard

money he has brought in. Speaking of comparisons with Ray Robinson, let it be known that this great fighter got only 40,000 dollars on his biggest "pay day." Leonard pulled in close to ten million dollars for his one fight with Tommy Hearns. Case closed. As a fighter, though, Leonard is not just a television "freak". He comes as close in style, skill and guts to being on a par with the old timers as anyone could in this day and age. Its just that there are no Jake LaMottas, Rocky Grazianos, or Tommy Bells around. But there was one Roberto Duran, and I would be remiss not to mention his name. Save for the disgrace in New Orleans against Leonard, this little man from Panama carved out a nice niche for himself with his granite fists. As Casey Stengel used to say, "You could look it up."

What is the Record for Most Knockdowns in One Round?

The answer to this one brings us back to the Dempsey-Firpo fight, considered by many experts to have been the fiercest battle ever fought. It lasted two rounds, with Dempsey crushing the Wild Bull of the Pampas to the canvas seven times in the first three minutes. During those 180 seconds, Dempsey came within a whisker of losing his title when he was knocked out of the ring while a crowd of 90,000 at the Polo Grounds went into a wild uproar. In all, there were nine knockdowns in the first round. Firpo went down three more times in the second round as Dempsey, springing to the attack the instant the courageous Argentine rose, pummeled him savagely.

What is the Record for Most Knockdowns in a Fight?

Would you believe 49? It's hard to imagine two men having the stamina to last through so many knockdowns, but Battling Nelson, the great Danish

Jack Dempsey climbs back through the ropes after having been knocked through them by Luis Angel Firpo. In a dramatic follow-up, Dempsey went on to win this heavyweight-championship bout by a knockout.

lightweight champion, floored Christy Williams 42 times and hit the deck seven times himself before he put Williams away in the seventeenth round in a nontitle bout on December 26, 1902.

Williams shares the record for most knockdowns suffered by one fighter with Jack Havlin, who did the bouncing act over 29 rounds against Tommy Warren in San Francisco on September 25, 1888, when men were men. Warren never so much as smudged his trunks.

Which Fighter Holds the Record for Most Knockouts?

Dapper, mustachioed Archie Moore, who had 226 bouts and won more than half of them—138—by knockouts. Moore started his career in 1936, but not until late in his career, in 1952, did he get a crack at a title, beating Joey Maxim for the light-heavyweight crown. He fought Rocky Marciano for the heavyweight title in 1955 and was knocked out in the ninth round. He retired in 1964.

A knockdown, while not always a prelude to a knockout, is a good measure of how soon a knockout might occur. Many fights have had many knockdowns, and in one real donny-brook, with both fighters hitting the canvas frequently, it was not the outcome that was in doubt, but which fighter would score a knockout first.

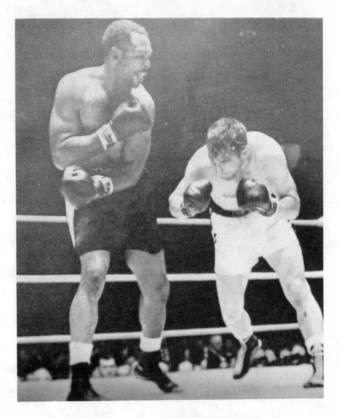

Archie Moore batters Yvonne Durelle of Canada en route to retaining the light-heavyweight title.

What Was the Longest Glove Fight on Record?

Can you imagine two men belting each other for 110 rounds, a total of seven hours and 19 minutes, and nobody winning? That's what the two "gentlemen," Andy Bowen and Jack Burke, did on April 6, 1893, at New Orleans. The fight was called a draw by the referee when neither man could continue.

How Are Fights Scored?

In different parts of the United States there are several ways of scoring a bout. In New York State, the referee and the judges score the fight on both a round-by-round and a point system. If a bout ends in a draw on the basis of rounds, then the officials revert to their point scores to determine a winner. The point system ranges from 1 to 4. A fighter's display of basic tactics is taken into account, and if he wins a round by a slim margin he gets a point, the loser zero; a decisive round will earn two points; a one-sided round or one in which a knockdown has been scored will earn three points; and a one-sided round with two or more knockdowns, four points.

In most states affiliated with the National Boxing Association, the five-point must system is the rule. That is, a fighter winning a round, even if only by a shade, will get five points. A knockdown and a clear superiority in a round will give the winner a 5-to-3 margin, and so forth. In a similar way a ten-point must system is used in Massachusetts, Ohio, Texas, and Miami Beach.

New Jersey uses a rounds system (no points). In California a five-point system is in effect, but the winner can receive anywhere from one to five points, the loser zero. It's not uncommon for a round to be scored 0-0.

As you can see, there's a lot to be said for the knockout. It does away with all that arithmetic, it settles the issue once and for all, and there is something infinitely satisfying in seeing someone twice as big as you stretched out on the canvas.

Here are some fast questions and answers to challenge you.

What Was the Largest Live Gate in Boxing History?

The second Dempsey-Tunney fight at Soldiers Field, Chicago. The gate was $2,658,660! And remember, there was no TV money in those days! The time was 1927.

What Was the Largest Live Attendance at a Fight?

The first Dempsey-Tunney fight at Sesqui-Centennial Stadium, Philadelphia, September 23, 1926. The attendance was 120,757. On August 18, 1941, Tony Zale and Billy Pryor fought before 135,132 in Milwaukee, at the Fraternal Order of Eagles Free Show.

How Many Fighters Have Never Been Defeated in a Pro Career?

Four, Rocky Marciano (1947–1955), 49 fights; Jack McAuliffe (1884–1897), 53 bouts; Larry Foley (1886–1888), 22 fights; Jimmy Barry (1891–1899), 70 bouts.

Who Refereed the Most Title Bouts?

Yes, referees set records, too. Arthur Donovan refereed fourteen title fights in the boxing ring.

Who Was the Youngest Fighter to Win a Heavyweight title?

Floyd Patterson, at 21, was the youngest fighter to win a heavyweight title. Two other youngsters who did it were Cassius Clay (22) and Joe Louis (23). Jersey Joe Walcott was the oldest, at 37.

Jacques Plante (left) and Maurice ("Rocket") Richard pose with the coveted Stanley Cup, emblematic of world hockey supremacy.

HOCKEY

If you're under the impression that only in the United States do they debate origins of sports, rest easy. The quickest way to get two Canadians into a debate is to ask, "Where did hockey get started?" I said quickest, but I should have added that it ought to be a Canadian from Western Canada and one from Eastern Canada.

When the governing officials of hockey decided that a Hall of Fame was needed, their plan for getting a site was based on giving it to that community which could best show that it indeed was the birthplace of the game. Three very strong bids were made by Montreal, Kingston and Halifax. The Canadian Amateur Hockey Association then appointed a committee to render a decision. They came to the conclusion that Kingston, Ontario had the strongest claim. The committee traced the game in Kingston back to 1855. The first players were members of Her Majesty's Royal Canadian Rifles. There were some who made an even prior claim to the game's having been played as early as the 1830's.

Montreal did not take to the decision without some rancor. Those who opted for Montreal claimed that the first true game of ice hockey was played in Montreal in 1875 by teams of students from McGill University. But there were complications here, because if you accepted the story that students at McGill had started the game, then there seemed to be some evidence that one of those students, J.G.A. Creighton, brought it to the campus from his home town of Halifax. And that's where it stood.

Then National Hockey League officials approached the leaders of the Canadian National Exhibition in Toronto, where Canada's Sports Hall of Fame had been established, and that's where the Hockey Hall of Fame was installed.

Which Was the First Hockey League?

As you might expect, the first hockey league revolved around Kingston. There were four teams in the league established at Kingston in 1885—the Royal Military College, Queen's University, the Kingston Athletics and the Kingston Hockey Club. The Queen's University players were the first champions.

Which Came First, the National Hockey League or the Stanley Cup?

The Stanley Cup. That may seem strange to those who have the impression that first came the National Hockey League and then came the Stanley Cup. It's just the other way around. The Stanley Cup preceded the National Hockey League by quite a few years. It was first presented to the team winning the championship of Canada in 1893. The National Hockey League came into existence in 1917. So there's a time span of 24 years. The Stanley Cup came into being as a result of the interest not of Lord Stanley, the Governor General, but of his aide, Lord Kilcoursie. It seems that Lord Kilcoursie had become quite a hockey enthusiast, and at his suggestion Lord Stanley of Preston donated the prize. The first winner was the Montreal A.A.A. team.

Which Were the First Teams in the N.H.L.?

The National Hockey League, an outgrowth of the National Hockey Association, was organized November 22, 1817, in Montreal. It was composed of the Montreal Canadiens, the Montreal Wanderers, Ottawa, Quebec, and the Toronto Arenas. Quebec did not operate that season. Later in 1918, when the Westmount Arena, home of the Wanderers, burned, the team dropped out of existence.

Which Was the First United States Team?

In 1924, the Boston Bruins became the first United States team. Then the New York Americans came into the league, followed by the Pittsburgh Pirates, both in 1925. In 1926, the New York Rangers, the Chicago Black Hawks and the Detroit Cougars were admitted.

What is the Hart Memorial Trophy?

This is an annual award made to the player adjudged to be most valuable to his team. The winner is selected in a poll by the Professional Hockey Writers association in the twenty-one NHL cities at the end of the regular schedule. The winner receives $1,500 and the runner-up gets $750.

The Hart Memorial Trophy was presented by the National Hockey League in 1960 after the original Hart Trophy was retired to the Hockey Hall of Fame. The original Hart Trophy was donated to the NHL in 1923 by Dr. David A. Hart, father of Cecil Hart, the former manager-coach of the Montreal Canadiens. The first winner was Frank Nighbor of the Ottawa team. Gordy Howe, an all-time great, has won this award more times than any other player—six times he was chosen most valuable. Eddie Shore, another great, won the award on four different occasions. Howe, Shore, the late great Howie Morenz, Bobby Hull, Stan Mikita, Bobby Clark, Guy Lafleur and Wayne Gretzky have all won it back to back. Gretzky, the current wonder kid, is the only player ever to win the trophy in his first two seasons. Finally, the fabulous Bobby Orr won it three years in a row.

Bill Chadwick (right), hockey's most famous referee, with Clarence Campbell, president of the National Hockey League.

Eddie Shore

What is the Art Ross Trophy?

This annual award is given to the player who leads the league in scoring. The overall winner receives $1,000. The overall runner-up $500. The leader at the end of the first half of the season and the leader of the second half each receive $500. The runners-up in each half get $250. The award was presented to the NHL in 1947 by Arthur Howie Ross, the former manager-coach of the Boston Bruins. If two players finish the season with the same number of points, the trophy is awarded to the player with the most goals. If they have the same number of goals, then the player with the fewer games gets it. If they've played the same number of games, then it's the one who scored first during the season. The first scoring leader was Joe Malone of the Montreal Canadiens in 1918. The man who has won this award the most times is the same player who has won the Hart Trophy most, Gordie Howe. Six times the big forward outscored every one in the league. The next period of dominance came with the emergence of Phil Esposito as a superstar. It was he who became the first man ever to score more than 100 points in a season. The record for points had been 97, held jointly by the two great Chicago Black Hawk stars, Bobby Hull, the Golden Jet, and Stan Mikita. Mikita, incidentally, led the league in scoring four times, and Hull three. But

89

in 1969, Esposito with 49 goals and 77 assists totalled 126 points. He didn't break the record—he destroyed it. And it was only the beginning. In 1970 he set the all time record for goals in a season with 76. He added 76 assists for an unbelievable 152 points. But don't go away. Wayne Gretzky was yet to come. This incredible youngster in 1981 put together 55 goals and 109 assists for a total of 164 points. Even as this is being written, one wonders . . . will the record hold up? With the likes of Gretzky, Bryan Trottier, Marcel Dionne, Mike Bossy, and Guy Lafleur, can a new record be far away? One should take note that in his first four seasons Bossy has averaged over sixty goals a season. A staggering statistic. One should also note that in the long history of the league there never had been a defenseman who scored over 100 points until the coming of Bobby Orr. This great player produced 139 points in one season for his all time high. Had injuries not withered him, who knows what further records he might have set? Suffice it to say that with the addition of great players from Sweden, Czechoslovakia, and Finland and with the remote possibility of some of Russia's greats, hockey fans are in for many future exploits of excellence. Who would have thought a defenseman would score over forty goals? Bobby Orr did. Who would have thought that one

Mike Bossy,
the scoring machine.

Bobby Orr

man would total 85 goals in a season, including playoffs? Mike Bossy did. The list goes on and on. From the time that Joe Malone handed the baton to Howie Morenz who handed it to Charlie Conacher, who gave it to the fabulous Maurice ("Rocket") Richard, to Gordie Howe to Bobby Hull to Phil Esposito to Guy Lafleur and on to Mike Bossy the results have exceeded the expectations by incredible leaps and bounds. As we go into the 80's, the explosion continues.

What is the James Norris Memorial Trophy?

This award is given annually to the defenseman who demonstrates throughout the season the greatest all-around ability in that position. The winner is selected in a poll by the Professional Hockey Writers' Association. The winner gets $1500 and the runner-up $750. The award is made in memory of the late James Norris, former owner-president of the Detroit Red Wings.

This is the newest of the NHL achievement awards, having first been presented in 1953. Since that time, two defensemen claimed it as practically their personal property. They are Doug Harvey and Bobby Orr. Harvey was a great defenseman with the Montreal Canadiens. He was the first player at that position to control the tempo of a game. While his team, the Montreal Canadiens, had such great stars as Maurice Richard, Elmer Lach, Joe Blake, Jean Beliveau and many others, it was Harvey who set the pace of the game by the way he controlled the puck. Seven times he won the Norris Trophy for his outstanding play. And then along came Bobby Orr to elevate the standard even higher. The fact that Orr won the Norris Trophy eight consecutive years before injuries forced him to the sidelines, should be sufficient evidence. But there is more. Orr not only controlled the puck, but was a scoring machine. Certainly the greatest "offensive" defenseman skater in the history of hockey. Before you argue with that, ask yourself if you ever saw anyone who could shift gears like he could. And if you never saw him you missed an extraordinary talent.

Doug Harvey

I would be remiss not to mention Eddie Shore. The only reason he never won the Norris Trophy is because there was none when he played. Shore combined many of the talents of both Harvey and Orr. But he played at a time when convention dictated that a defenseman never leave his own blue-line. The chore "took-off" on his own and made some stunning solo rushes, and probably paved the way for those who came after. He was a great one.

Mention should also be made of two defenseman who have won the trophy three times. Pierre Pilote, whose coach in the minor leagues told him that he was too slow to make it to the big time, was the league's premier defenseman after Doug Harvey. He won the Norris Trophy three times. When Bobby Orr retired, it looked like Denis Potvin would be the man who would carry that mantle of greatness. Potvin, up to this point has won the trophy three times but injuries have kept him from total fulfillment. More than anyone else, he epitomizes the total defenseman. He is a devastating checker. His size makes that possible. And on offense, there has never been a defenseman who could pass the puck better. He ranks at the top of the list with Orr and Harvey.

What is the Vezina Trophy?

This award is given annually to the goal keeper or goal keepers for the team with the fewest goals scored against it. The overall winner receives $1500 and the runner-up $750. The leaders at the end of the first and second halves of the season, respectively, receive $250. This award is presented in

Jacques Plante ready to stop a goal.

memory of Georges Vezina, the great goal tender of the Canadiens who collapsed during a game and died a few months later. He had contracted tuberculosis. The winners of this award read like a "who's who" of goal-tending. Actually, though, it has been a Montreal Canadiens goal tender who usually wins it. Notice that Bill Durnan won it six times, Jacques Plante also won it six times with the Canadiens, and Ken Dryden five times. The record is held by Plante who won it a seventh time while with the St. Louis Blues. You might ask does this make Plante the greatest of all goal tenders? Hardly. That distinction has been argued about since the time of Vezina himself. While Plante was a great innovator—he is generally credited with being the first roving goalie—there are others whose ability to keep the puck out of the net was exemplary. The first name which comes to mind is that of Terry Sawchuk. He posted the most shutouts by a goalie—103. Many thought he had no peer. Others said the same of Glenn Hall. He was not a classic stand-up style of goalkeeper. Sometimes he "flopped" to the ice, but in a fashion that enabled him to recover quickly. He was outstanding. Old-timers always mention Tiny Thompson of the Boston Bruins. The greatest catching-hand of them all. And how about George Hainsworth?

Good enough to put 94 shutouts next to his name. And let's not forget the man they called "Mr. Zero". His name . . . Frank Grimsek. The list goes on. I've obviously overlooked some. Were you thinking of Chuck Gardiner? Or Turk Broda? Or Harry Lumley? Or Tony Esposito? They all deserve a place in the pantheon of greatness. You know, I almost forgot Bernie Parent. The greatest? Maybe he's the one just coming up on the horizon.

What is the Lady Byng Trophy?

There is something most unique about this award. Hockey is considered by some to be the roughest sport played. The Lady Byng Trophy is given to the player who is adjudged to have exhibited the best type of sportsmanship and gentlemanly conduct combined with a high standard of playing ability. The winner of the award, chosen by the N.H.L. Writers' Association, gets $1,500 and the runner-up $750.

This award was first presented in 1925 by Lady Byng, the wife of Canada's Governor-General at the time. After Frank Boucher of the New York Rangers won the award seven times in eight seasons, he was given the trophy to keep and Lady Byng donated another trophy. Boucher, who was the center for the great Ranger line that included the immortal Cook brothers, Bill and Bun, is the player most associated with this particular award. What is interesting is that in recent years a player as aggressive as Stan Mikita of the Chicago Black Hawks has been able to win the award. There are some players, of course, to whom this award is of no great consequence. Gordie Howe, perhaps the greatest all-around player of all time, has always said that this trophy held no great fascination for him.

Who is Hockey's Greatest Player?

Just as in any other sport, the choice of "greatest" will get you into a debate. But in this sport, the choice may be a bit easier. Look at it this way. If you are going to pick the greatest what would be the yardstick? You'd think in terms of offense and defense plus length of service. When those measurements are used the answer really is pretty obvious. The name of the player has to be Gordie Howe. He has scored more points than any player in history. Mind you there have been more prolific goal scorers if you go season by season. Phil Esposito immediately pops to mind. And Mike Bossy scored the most goals ever by a right winger, Howe's position. Matter of fact Gordie never scored 50 goals in a season. But when you look at the National Hockey League record for most points . . . there it is. 1,850 by Gordie Howe. And that doesn't include the points Gordie got while playing in the World Hockey Association. And it is not only offense. He could play defense—and he could handle the puck—and he could take the body. In a sport where roughness and toughness is a fact of life, no one was rougher or tougher than Gordie Howe. The man won the Hart and Ross Trophies more than anyone and at an age when the rocking chair beckoned, he became one of the first players to break the 100-point mark.

There have been others to rival him. In his peak years, Howe's greatest adversary was the great Maurice ("Rocket") Richard. Howe did more. Bobby Orr could skate faster, but unlike Howe he became vulnerable to the rigors of the sport and had to retire. And that really sums it up. Howe did it great for a longer time than anyone. Come to think of it, no one in any other sport rivals him.

Gordie Howe scoring the five-hundreth goal of his career.

Who Was the Most Exciting Hockey Player?

I suppose the answer to this might depend on what team you rooted for. But in general if you were to say "Rocket" Richard of the Montreal Canadiens, the "Golden Jet," Bobby Hull of the Chicago Black Hawks, or Bobby Orr of the Boston Bruins, you wouldn't be far from right. For eighteen seasons Joseph Henri Maurice Richard, better known as the "Rocket," put on his twelve pounds of shin and shoulder pads, ankle-length underwear, skates, and stove-pipe pants to maintain his position as the most exciting player around. He was a demigod to his French-Canadian followers, a king, the goal-scoring nonpareil, the most dynamic and dramatic star in professional hockey. Richard scored his final goal for the Montreal Canadiens in the 1960 Stanley Cup play-offs. It was his 82nd in the Stanley Cup, a record, and it raised his lifetime total to 626.

On November 9, 1952, when the Rocket tallied his 325th goal, he became the National Hockey League's highest individual scorer in history. The puck was sent to Queen Elizabeth of England.

Richard had a fiery temper that caused many an incident around the league. A stiff penalty imposed on Richard prompted the infamous Montreal riot of March 17, 1955, wherein unhappy fans capsized streetcars, broke store windows, and pelted the league president with assorted rancid grocery articles. Only an impassioned plea by Richard himself on radio and TV quieted them.

Maurice ("Rocket") Richard

Richard was strictly a one-way player. The arrow always pointed toward the other team's goalie. He once scored five goals and three assists in a game.

But the best indication of this man's attitude can be seen in a story told by hockey referee Bill Chadwick. Years after Chadwick had retired from the game he asked Richard for an autograph for his son. "Why should I give it to you?" asked Richard. "All you ever did for me was give me penalties!"

That's not the case for Robert Marvin Hull. There never was or will be a hockey player more conscious of what he considered his responsibility to the public than the "Golden Jet." Bobby Hull was like Babe Ruth. The fans everywhere loved him and he loved them. Watching a crowd at the Boston Gardens cheer Hull who was there only to serve as a television commentator, epitomizes how even rival fans reacted to his dynamic charisma. It wasn't just that he scored a goal. It was the way he scored a goal. He loved to play and he loved to smile. There were those who complained that if Bobby Hull were only a little meaner, he'd be greater. If you had told that to Bobby, he would have laughed and said, "I'm trying to beat them, not kill them." Be that as it may, when Hull bore down on a goal tender and let the shot go at a 120 miles an hour, the goalie often wondered whether safety would have been wiser. Those who saw Bobby will never forget how during the season of 1968–69 when he set the then record total of 58 goals in a season, he played a good portion of that season with a broken jaw that had to be wired. It made eating very difficult and when you can't eat, you're not quite as strong. But even below normal strength, Hull was a marvel.

At 5' 10", 198 pounds, with the arms of a Neanderthal man and the torso of a weight lifter, and with the golden locks, Hull on skates was a sight never to be forgotten.

Robert Gordon Orr belongs in the same league with Richard and Hull. The strangest part of it all is that while Richard and Hull were forwards and Orr a defenseman, Bobby Orr was not as physical a player. But don't let that fool you. When Orr was in his prime, some old timers complained that if they had been playing they would have stopped Orr by hitting him with their bodies. It brought a round of laughs. Hit Orr . . . what a joke. You had to catch him to hit him and no one could catch him. He had the most incredible gear shift in the history of the sport. Just when you came close to him he would shift to a higher speed. There were players with great speed themselves who bitterly complained that Orr had "after-burners." The irony was that the great legs which produced this speed ultimately betrayed him. His knees went bad. Even modern sports medicine couldn't save him. But while he played he could lug the puck as no one ever had. He would rush it from one end of the rink to the other with bursts that were breath-taking.

Richard, Hull, Orr. They had charisma.

What is Unusual About Bill Chadwick?

Bill Chadwick may be the greatest referee the sport of hockey has ever had. In a sport dominated by Canadians, Bill Chadwick is unusual in that he is from the United States. But even that doesn't tell the whole story. What is most unusual about Bill Chadwick is that while he was an active official, he had only partial sight. As a youngster, while playing hockey in his native New York City, Bill was the victim of an accident that robbed him of practically all vision in one eye. Despite this handicap, Chadwick, with the sanction of the governors of the National Hockey League, worked and became a great hockey official.

What Was the Origin of Hockey in the United States?

In 1893, two Yale tennis champions, Malcolm G. Chace and Arthur E. Foote, started the sport on the New Haven campus. The game quickly spread throughout the nation. Three years later the Amateur Hockey League was formed in New York and a league was started in Baltimore. The rise of the professional game stimulated amateur interest. Presently there are more than three hundred teams, including many in the N.C.A.A., registered with the Amateur Hockey Association.

Ice hockey first became part of the Olympic schedule in the 1929 games in Amsterdam. Canada, because of its experience in the sport, emerged with the goal medals in 1920, 1924, 1928, and 1932. The British broke the string in 1936.

Can U.S. Teams Produce National Hockey League Players?

When this question was first asked, there was still some skepticism. No more. Not after the incredible victory by the United States Olympic Hockey Team over the famed Russians in 1980. With that victory, hockey in the U.S. soared to a plateau never before reached. Sure, there have been American players in the National Hockey League for a long time, but they were rare birds. Now, all one has to do is look at the roster of the Minnesota North Stars, a Stanley Cup finalist, in 1981. Fifteen of the players listed are American born and they include some of the league's best. While Minnesota, a hot bed of hockey, is more American than other teams in the NHL, more and more teams are becoming peopled with American players. There is no reason why this shouldn't be so. All it ever took was interest. It might also be pointed out that this game of hockey which used to be considered Canadian, has now become so international in scope that the Soviet Union is now laying claim to being the capital of hockey. What does it all mean? Just better hockey.

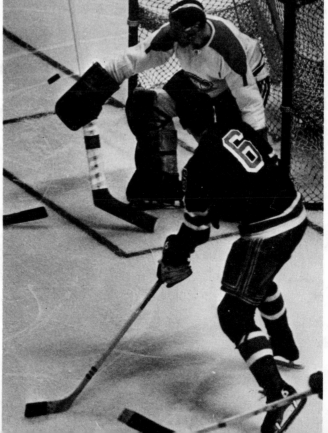

This National Hockey League game was won by the Montreal Candiens whose goalie, Jacques Plante, is shown here successfully fending off a shot attempted by the New York Rangers.

Francis Ouimet shaking hands with Harry Vardon (left) and Ted Ray (right), his opponents in the 1913 U.S. Open Golf Championship. Ouimet scored one of the game's biggest upsets by winning.

GOLF

You can have more fun talking about the beginnings of the game of golf than about any other sport. Somewhere, someone wrote that Adam actually was the first golfer. It seems that he made a club from one of his ribs—and Eve thus became the first golf widow.

There is the group that always refers to horse racing as the sport of kings. You could get a good argument from golf historians who will say that royalty has indulged in golf, too. And quite a few notables of history were addicted to the pursuit of the little ball around green pastures. Some historians seriously claim that shepherds tending flocks of sheep in ancient times were the first to apply a stick to a ball, or more accurately, a club to the ball.

100

But there seems little doubt that the game as we know it today was first played by the Scots. Golf is known to have been popular around 1440, so popular that James II took a dislike to what the people were doing and prevailed upon Parliament to enact a rule during the month of March making it unlawful to play the game.

Then along came James IV, and he took enough of a liking to the game to indulge in it himself, becoming a fair player. His son, James V, didn't play, but neither did he stop anyone.

The first lady golfer was apparently Mary, Queen of Scots. With her appearance on the links the game took a real stride forward. It was during her reign (about 1552) that St. Andrews, the most famous of golf clubs, was founded.

Apparently, there were no Ben Hogans, Arnold Palmers or players of that caliber at that time, because there are no reports about them. If there were any great players, they played in private. But that seems impossible. Have you ever heard of a silent golfer? Come to think of it, I've heard of one named Willie Anderson. More about Willie Anderson later.

When Did the British Open Start?

In 1860, a tournament was held at the Prestwick Club in Scotland which was the beginning of the British Open. Willie Park, Sr. and Tom Morris, Sr. dominated the game. Between them they won the first five tournaments; Morris won three times and Park twice.

Tom Morris, Jr. won in 1868, 1869 and 1870. Then there was a halt in playing for several years. It didn't have any effect on Morris, because when playing resumed in 1872, this young man, a truly fine player, again won the title. In a time when the gutta-percha ball was played, Tom Morris, Jr. shot a 149 for 36 holes. No one ever shot better with the solid gutta-percha ball.

As for the beginnings of the game in North America, there are mentions of golf clubs having existed in South Carolina and Georgia during the eighteenth century, but there is no record of play. Some historians say that Scottish regiments stationed there were the first to play the game.

The game as we now know it was first played in the 1880's, however. A gentleman named Joseph Mickle Fox, a Philadelphian, learned about the game on a trip to Scotland, and when he returned he introduced it at his summer home. This led to the founding of the Foxburg Golf Club in 1887. That would make the club about the oldest in the United States.

When Did the U.S. Open Start?

It was started in 1894 at a course known as St. Andrews Golf Club in Yonkers, N.Y., which seems like poetic justice. The Yonkers club came into being as a result of the work of John Reid, who has been credited as the father of American golf. Mr Reid was a transplanted Scotsman, and it was at a dinner party given for a group of his friends that the St. Andrews Golf Club was conceived. It was on that course in 1894 that Willie Dunn defeated Willie Campbell two-up to win the first U.S. Open.

When Was the United States Golf Association Formed?

In the same year that the first U.S. Open was played, the U.S. Golf Association was born. Clubmen decided that an official organization was needed and that rules should be set forth, including stipulations regarding amateurs and pros in the sport. And so was born the U.S.G.A.

When Was the First Amateur Championship Played?

This event took place in 1895, and the first United States amateur champion was a gentleman named C.B. MacDonald. Mr. MacDonald beat C.E. Sands by the comfortable margin of 12 and 11 (12 holes up with 11 to play). The next day they played the U.S. Open on the same course at Newport. This time it was medal play instead of match play. In medal play you just count strokes, while in match play you play hole by hole. When Willie Dunn had won the first open in 1894, it was match play. This time, at medal play, the winner, Horace Rawlins, shot 173 for 36 holes.

When Did the Ladies Start their Championship?

Women had taken an interest in the game from the time that it was introduced in Yonkers, and so when the men said they were going to have an amateur championship, the ladies decided they wanted one, too. The U.S.G.A. women's amateur championship came into being in 1895. There were thirteen contestants at the new Meadow Brook Club course on Long Island to determine a women's champion. It was medal play and Mrs. C. S. Brown was the winner with a total of 132 shots for 18 holes—not exactly inspiring. The next year it was changed to match play, and it has stayed that way since.

Who Were Vardon and Ray?

It sounds like the name of a cough drop unless you really know your golf. If you do, then you know that Harry Vardon and Ted Ray were two players from England who made a terrific impact on the game in the United States. Harry Vardon made the more lasting one because it was his grip on the golf club, the Vardon grip, which is the most popular golf grip known. They tell the story that Vardon's greatest difficulty in playing the game was that the second day he played on a golf course, he would be hitting the ball out of his own divots. You all know, of course, that a divot is a bit of turf knocked out of the ground by the club when you hit a golf shot. After the shot, the turf is replaced. Vardon won the British championship six times and the American title once. As for his compatriot, Ted Ray, he was a brute of a player who knocked the cover off the ball with every swing; and when one mentions divots, the ones that Ray took were the size of throw rugs. These two men played the game in an opposite manner. Ray was the home-run hitter, Vardon was the stylist.

What Young American Beat Vardon and Ray?

There was one player in it who had grown up right across the way from the Country Club. His name was Francis Ouimet. If you had ever breathed his name in the same company as Harry Vardon and Ted Ray, knowledgeable golfers would have thought you were out of your mind.

So it was that at the end of the first 36 holes of play, Vardon and another Englishman, a fellow named Reid, were tied at 147. Ted Ray was two shots behind. At 151 was twenty-year-old Francis Ouimet, and he was tied with another twenty-year-old by the name of Walter Hagen.

Well, when the third round of play was over, there was a tremendous surprise. Oh, sure, Vardon and Ray were out in front at 225, but there was another 225 up there on the board and it belonged to Francis Ouimet. Over that rain-drenched course Ouimet had fashioned a 74.

Well, sir, on that final day Ted Ray and Harry Vardon came home in 79 and they were in a tie at 304. But where was Francis Ouimet? Still out on the golf course, that's where he was. When he got to the thirteenth hole, he was in a tough spot. He needed two birdies on the last six holes just to get a tie.

At thirteen, Ouimet chipped in from off the green for one of those two birdies. At fourteen, fifteen and sixteen, he had to settle for pars. Two holes to go and he desperately needed another birdie for the tie. On seventeen he drove well and knocked his second shot up on the green. It was a tough putt that he needed to get the birdie. It was asking too much of a great player, much less an inexperienced twenty-year-old. But Francis knocked the putt in the cup and he had his birdie. Now all he needed was a par four on the last hole and he'd have a tie with Vardon and Ray.

Ouimet drove the ball well, but his second shot was just short of the green. He set himself for the chip. He wanted to get it as close as he could for a gimme putt. But his approach was left five feet away. A really tough putt on any day . . . and on a day like this it must have seemed a dream away. But

104

the dream became a reality, because Ouimet never hesitated. He walked up, took a quick look at the line, and knocked it in. Just like that, he knocked it in. Like you'd do it any old time. He was tied with Vardon and Ray.

The next day, the day of the playoff, it rained. But they played, the two great English pros and the skinny twenty-year-old amateur. And how they played! It was as if destiny were riding on the wrong horse. Not the trained, skilled ones, but the young one, the inexperienced one.

They were all even at the end of nine holes, but on number ten, Ouimet picked up a shot on both Vardon and Ray when they three-putted for fours while he was down in par three. Now the Englishmen started to press. On the fifteenth hole, Ted Ray took a six on a par-four hole. He was now slipping out of contention. But there was still the incomparable Harry Vardon. At seventeen, Vardon too showed the wear and tear by bogeying the hole while Ouimet got a birdie. That was it. It was all over but the shouting. On the last hole Vardon took a double bogey, and although Ray had a birdie, they both had had it. Vardon had finished with 77, Ray with 78, and here was Ouimet running in his final putt for a round of 72. A twenty-year-old American had reserved a page in golf history for himself. From that day on, Francis Ouimet was a golfing immortal.

What About the Other Twenty-Year-Old, Walter Hagen?

If there was one player who made a greater mark on the game of golf than Walter Hagen, you'll have to prove it. No, he wasn't the best of all, but he was right up there with any of them. But even if he hadn't been that great a player, he was still something else, as they say. It was Walter Hagen, more than any other professional, who took the professionals from the back door entrance and got them to walk in the front door. That's who Walter Hagen was. He could have been a major-league baseball player if he had been so inclined. He was that good an athlete. But he wanted to do it as a golfer. And he did it.

Walter Hagen, playing his game at Fresh Meadow Country Club in 1939.

He came out of Rochester, N.Y. He was brash, maybe even cocky. They say that when he got to Brookline in 1913, he walked up to the defending champion, Johnny McDermott, and said, "I've come to help you take care of Vardon and Ray." It was Ouimet who won it, but at the end of 72 holes Hagen was only three shots back and it was a triple bogey at the fourteenth hole that stopped him. It was only a momentary detour. If you will check the record book, you'll see that the winner of the U.S. Open the next year, in 1914, was Walter Hagen. He won the U.S. Open again in 1919. Then he went across the sea and won the British Open four times. Note, too, that he won the P.G.A. championship on five occasions. He won the P.G.A. four times in a row, and it's likely that no one will ever tie that mark.

What of Hagen's Great Match with Bobby Jones?

In 1926, Hagen was a little upset about the fact that a young amateur named Bobby Jones was being accclaimed as the greatest golfer in the world. In his typical fashion he figured that something like the "greatest golfer in

Bobby Jones displaying his long driving style.

the world" title should be decided on a golf course. He got a friend to arrange a match with Jones. They were to play seventy-two holes. Thirty-six would be played at Bobby Jones's course and thirty-six at Hagen's. It was no contest—the Haig beat Jones twelve and eleven. It was the worst defeat ever suffered by Bobby Jones.

107

What is Bobby Jones Most Famous For?

Walter Hagen once said, "If I were asked to vote for the greatest golfer of all time, my vote would go to Bobby Jones." When he said it, he was probably thinking most about what Jones had done in 1930. In that year, Bobby Jones did something no one else had ever done, has ever done since, or probably will ever do. He made the "Grand Slam" of golf. He won the U.S. Amateur, the U.S. Open, the British Amateur and the British Open!

It started with the British Amateur. His toughest match here was against the defending champion, Cyril Tolley, whom he beat one up in nineteen holes. In the final he beat Roger Wethered 7 and 6.

At the British Open he shot 291 to win. He now had two legs on the "Grand Slam."

Back to the United States he came. First it was the Open, played at Interlaken in Minneapolis. He shot 71, 73, 68 and 75 for 287, and the U.S. Open was his.

The Merion Cricket Club was the setting for the National Amateur. It was just a triumphant tour. Jones had no match closer than 5 and 4, and in the final he beat Gene Homans 8 and 7.

That did it for Bobby Jones. He retired then and there at the age of 28. He had won thirteen major championships in eight years. He was known as "Emperor" Jones. He deserved the royal tag.

Which Player Won the U.S. Open by Playing the Last 28 Holes in 100 Strokes?

They call him the Squire. His name is Gene Sarazen, the most durable player the game has known. He trained around 1920, when still a teen-ager, and in the next fifteen years won two U.S. Opens, three P.G.A. championships, the British Open, and the Masters, plus dozens of other tournaments around the world. He tied for the U.S. Open in 1940, losing in a play-off. In

Gene Sarazen

his fifties he was still playing sub-par golf.

Now about those 100 shots on the last 28 holes. It took place at Fresh Meadow in 1932. On the final day Gene shot the last ten holes of the morning round in 34. That was like a warm-up, because on the final eighteen holes played in the afternoon he blasted out a 66. It was good enough.

Years later, three to be exact, he sank a 220-yard spoon shot that gave him a double eagle and a tie for the Masters which he won in a play-off with Craig Wood the next day. Sarazen made a specialty out of clutch wins.

How Great Was Byron Nelson?

There are those who will tell you that no one who ever played the game could hit the ball straighter than Lord Byron. With his picture swing, he'd strike that ball like he was mechanical.

Nelson played his greatest golf during the early 1940's, He was exempt from service in World War II because he suffered from hemophilia. Actually, Nelson started making his mark on the big-time trail in 1937. That year he won the Masters for the first time. In 1939, the National Open was his in a play-off with Denny Shute and Craig Wood. He won his first P.G.A. in 1940 by beating Sam Snead one up in 36 holes.

Then he won his second Masters in 1942 by outscoring Ben Hogan. But there was more to come. In the two-year period of 1944–45, Nelson was lord and master of all he surveyed. In 1944 Nelson won seven tournaments, and in 1945 he won 19 tournaments, 11 in a row. But his streak was just about over.

In talking about Byron Nelson there has always been a tendency to disparage because many of his wins were scored while some players were away in the service and because his career was rather short. Both of these attitudes are ill-deserved. Nelson did not choose his time, nor did he have control of the illness which hobbled him. In a game where style is a major factor, this man must be rated as one of the greatest stylists of them all.

What About Ben Hogan?

I first saw Hogan play at the Western Open in 1948. To win it, he had to beat Ed "Porky" Oliver in a play-off. Hogan shot 64. He won it. The next year, seemingly on his way to golf's greatest successes, Hogan almost lost his life. It was on February 2, 1949, on one of those lonely Texas highways, that Ben Hogan almost cashed his chips in. He was driving back to his home in Fort Worth on a hazy day when a bus bore down out of nowhere. Instinctively, Hogan flung himself in front of his wife to shield her as the bus and his car collided.

Valerie Hogan, thanks to her husband's heroic action, suffered only minor injuries, but Ben sustained a double fracture of the pelvis, a broken collar bone, a fractured left ankle, and a smashed right rib. He was taken to a hospital in El Paso and apparently was coming out of it all right when he developed a thrombosis (blood clot). In order to stop the clotting, doctors had to tie off the veins in his legs. They saved Hogan's life, but it seemed the end of his golfing career. It might have ended many careers. It didn't end Ben Hogan's.

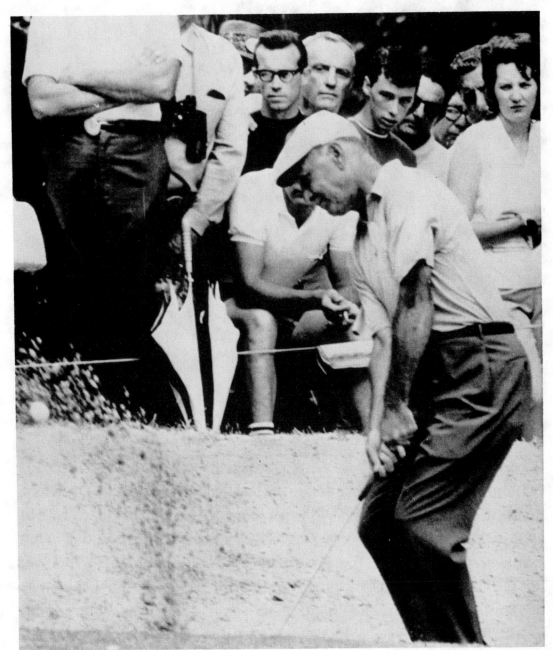

Ben Hogan blasting out of a wet sand trap.

Sam Snead

What is Considered Hogan's Greatest Feat?

There are those who might point to the fact that he won the U.S. Open four times. So did Bobby Jones and Willie Anderson. I lean toward what he did in 1953 as the highlight of his career. He hadn't been out of the hospital for too long when he won the U.S. Open in 1950. He repeated in 1951. In 1952, Julius Boros interrupted his string. Which brings us to 1953. First, there was the Masters. He shot rounds of 70-69-66-69 for 274. It was a tournament record. In the U.S. Open his total of 283 gave him an easy win—he finished six shots ahead of Sam Snead. Now there was the British Open. He had never been over to play in the British Open, and though his reputation had been established, there was still the matter of the winning of a crown that had graced the heads of great Americans like Hagen, Jones, and Sarazen. Besides which, those Scots had never seen him play. It was like going to the place of origin—so Hogan went. It was cold and rainy all the time. The ball being played, the English ball, was different, smaller, and the conditions on the course were unlike any that Hogan had ever been called upon to face.

But it was the time and the place for the Wee Ice Mon, as the Scots called Hogan. He didn't fail them or their faith in him. It was like a love affair, this feeling of Hogan and the Scots for one another. He proceeded to hammer out 73, 71, 70, and then a 68 for 282 and the British Open. In one year he had won the British and U.S. Opens *and* the Masters!

What Great Player Has Never Won the U.S. Open?

Even if you're not a big golf fan, you know the answer to this one, because everyone knows Sam Snead. Ask anyone, "Who's the hillbilly from West Virginia who plays golf?" and the answer comes back in torrents. That's how well-known Samuel Jackson Snead is. It really is amazing that this man, who has won well over a hundred tournaments in his life, has never won the Open . . . the U.S. Open, that is. He has won the British Open, and he has won the P.G.A. three times, and he has won the Masters three times, but in all the years he has played he has somehow managed to botch winning the U.S. Open. In his first try in 1937 he finished second to Ralph Guldahl. Everyone who saw him said, "Well, it's just a matter of time." Then, in 1939, he had something happen to him you wouldn't wish on anyone. He came to the last hole needing a five to win and a six to tie. He took an eight. In 1947, he lost in a play-off to Lew Worsham when he missed a little putt after Worsham had asked for a measurement to see who was away. Snead always said that there was no need for the measurement, that everyone could see he was away and should putt first. He was away, and he did putt first, and he missed, and Worsham didn't. Oh, yes, he finished second to Hogan in 1953.

Who is Golf's Most Charismatic Player?

Some old timers might say Walter Hagen and make a case for it. For me, though, the answer is simple—Arnold Palmer. If Hagen was able to bring the golfer from the back to the front door, Arnold Palmer made him the master of every home with a T.V. set. No performer ever commanded an audience more than Arnie. From the time he first appeared on television and hitched his pants, he was more than a golfer, he was a "star". No one has ever really explained what charisma is, but when you saw Palmer, you knew he had it. And he knew what to do with it. He made the touring pro into a business complex, a complex with many sidelines that went beyond golf. Arnold Palmer went from Hagen's Rolls-Royce to the jet airplane which he not only owned . . . but piloted. While no one can say for sure, it is estimated that he and Mohammed Ali have made the most money in their respective sports, close to one hundred million dollars. It all had its beginning with a sport and the televising of it.

Palmer made his first splash in the National Amateur. It was in 1954 that this bull-strong young man from Latrobe, Pennsylvania, won the title. He then joined the pro ranks. It took a while for the "army" to form, but suddenly all you heard in golf was, "Where's Palmer? How far behind is he?" Arnold Palmer brought the word "charge" into golf. Every Sunday on TV millions would tune in to watch Arnie make his charge. There was the Masters in 1960, for example.

Ken Venturi had come in at 283 and had gone to the clubhouse to try the traditional green jacket on for size—the jacket they give you at Augusta when you win. Out on the course, Arnold Palmer stood at seventeen. He needed a birdie on one of the last two holes for a tie. But seventeen and eighteen at Augusta aren't easy birdie holes. A drive and an eight iron left him 25 feet from the cup on 17. Palmer, with that mobile face, lined up his shot. The stroked putt went to the hole and fell in.

A birdie on 18 now and he would win it. As had always been the case before, and as it was to remain, Palmer played 18 with boldness. A tremendous drive, a whistling iron, and he was just five feet from victory. He waved

114

the wand—and there was another birdie in the cup. Ken Venturi had stopped trying coats on for size. In 1960, there was only one size—Arnold Palmer's.

How About the U.S. Open in 1960?

When talk gets around to famous charges that Arnold Palmer has made, you get your choice of quite a few. The one he made down the homestretch at the Cherry Hills course in Denver to win the Open was a classic, though. Going to the last eighteen holes, he was seven shots back of the leader, Big Mike Souchak. But don't get the impression that only Souchak was ahead of Arnie. There were fourteen other fine golfers in front of him, enough of a pack that it seemed only a miracle would do it—give Palmer his first Open win. All right, let's get out the magic wand and wave it. On the first hole, 346 yards, all Palmer did was drive the ball—right over the water and all, he drove it right on the green. Two putts and a birdie. Then, on the second hole, another birdie; and another on the third; and another on the fourth. On the fifth, Arnie had to settle for a par; but on six and seven, two more birdies. That opening barrage had brought a cluster of six birdies in seven holes. Although he bogied eight, his par on the ninth hole gave him a total of 30 for the first nine holes.

On the back nine he was able to fashion a 35 which, compared to his 30, may not seem magical, but his total of 65 was good enough to win him the U.S. Open.

Arnold Palmer

Who Do They Call the "Golden Bear"?

That name was tagged on Jack Nicklaus, the man many consider to be the greatest player of all time. No less an authority than Bobby Jones said of Nicklaus: "He plays another kind of game." From the time Nicklaus came out of Columbus, Ohio, as a young boy, he had the mark of greatness. While he wasn't able to pull off the "Grand Slam" as an amateur, he spread-eagled the amateur field as none other than Jones had been able to. At nineteen, he won the first of his two national amateurs. At twenty, playing in the world amateur championship at the Merion course near Philadelphia, Big Jack shot a 269. That total was 18 better than Hogan had used to win the National Open on the same course in 1950.

Jack Nicklaus putting.

116

Consider this. At this writing, Jack has won five P.G.A. titles, three British Opens, five Masters, and four U.S. Opens. No one has come close to that kind of mastery. What Nicklaus can do is drive the ball straighter and farther than any one and he can putt, repeat, he can really putt. I have heard it said that in the history of the game no one player ever had the artistry with the club like Leo Diegel. I've even heard one old-timer exclaim, "Nicklaus could never do what Diegel did". I asked the man, "Why didn't Diegel win the titles Nicklaus has?" "He couldn't putt". Then he burst out laughing. "Do you know, no matter how you cut it, there never has been a player like Nicklaus". And my friends, that about sums it up. There has never been a player like Jack Nicklaus.

Some years ago, Nicklaus was not the popular figure that he has since become. That probably was the result of his having come along and dethroned the great glamour figure—Arnold Palmer. It was not unlike the situation Gene Tunney found himself in after he beat Jack Dempsey. Tunney never was popular. But Jack Nicklaus not only became popular, but very well liked as a person. Some people say that it was a matter of changing his own image, literally.

You see when Jack first came on the scene he was rather heavy-set, and that's putting it mildly. That's where the bear of "Golden Bear", came from. But Nicklaus decided to change all that. He went on a diet and slimmed himself down considerably. He was a totally different man. But more than that, people began to recognize that Jack was really a very nice man. He wore his greatness with the modesty few have ever had. He was a total family man, too. None of this escaped notice and today Nicklaus, while not the glamour figure that Arnie Palmer was, is rooted for with great exuberance.

What Was Special About His Winning the U.S. Open?

Jack Nicklaus won the U.S. Open on his first try as a professional. It happened at the Oakmount course in 1962. Jack was all of 22 when he teed off in that competition, and the finish of it was something to see to believe. At the end of seventy-two holes, Nicklaus was in a tie with Arnold Palmer. Palmer at this time was the hottest player in the game. Those who were there and those who watched on television respected the Golden Bear, but against Arnold Palmer . . . forget it. No one was going to beat Arnie in the clutch. Nicklaus did, though. He beat Arnold Palmer that day—and then, a few weeks later when they met head-to-head in a 36-hole test for the televised World Series, Nicklaus did it again. As it turned out, Nicklaus was to be the chink in Arnie's armor, the fly in his ointment. Suddenly, where there had been one man with his feet on top of the golfing world, there were now two men astride and the younger one was pushing the other off, that younger one being Nicklaus.

Who Are Some of the Other Great Players?

The first name that comes to mind is that of Gary Player. Whenever you saw Nicklaus or Palmer, Player was not far behind. In spite of the fact that he is a relatively small man, the South African plays a big game. So did Billy Casper. When Billy first came on the scene, he was what you would call chubby. He went on a diet which included wild buffalo meat. Soon he was svelte. Something his game had always been. One has but to recall his head to head play-off against Arnold Palmer in 1966, for the U.S. Open. Casper won it. He had won the Open once before in 1959.

The name of Johnny Miller is added for two reasons. For one, he played a special brand of golf for several seasons and seemed ready to replace Jack Nicklaus as Nicklaus had replaced Arnold Palmer. No one knows, really knows, what went wrong on his way to super-stardom, but he never achieved it. Remember, I said two reasons . . . the second is that Miller, a tow-headed slender, all-American looking boy, seems to have spawned a whole procession of look-alikes. The most recent is a young man named Bill Rogers who at the moment seems ready to leap to the head of the class.

118

What Players Have Won Professional Golf's Grand Slam?

The Grand Slam in professional golf consists of the U.S. Open, the British Open, the Masters, and the P.G.A. There are only four men who've turned this trick—Ben Hogan, Gene Sarazen, Jack Nicklaus and Gary Player. No one has ever been able to do it in the same year.

What is the Longest Hole in One Ever Made?

Would you believe 444 yards? Robert Mitera of Omaha, Nebraska, knocked his tee shot into the cup on the tenth hole at the Miracle Hills Golf Club in Omaha. It took place on October 7, 1965, and it broke the old record which had been held by a former baseball player named Lou Kretlow. That mark had been a mere 427 yards. Incidentally, the odds of making a hole in one are listed at more than a million to one, so if you've never gotten a hole in one, don't feel bad.

What About the Women Golfers?

There is a popular advertising campaign which suggests "You've come a long way, baby." Let me tell you, the ladies sure have. There have always been great women golfers, but their reward was not much money-wise. Things sure have changed. The ladies on the tour today are making tremendous strides both in tour earnings and in outside commercial ventures. All you have to do is say Nancy Lopez Melton and the case is made. But let's take it in order and list some of the old timers, beginning with Joyce Wethered. Who was Joyce Wethered? It may surprise you to know that some golf experts say that she had the best swing ever in golf. And you never even heard of her. But ask those who saw her play, and they are unanimous in expressing the thought that this great English lady golfer was superior to even Sam Snead and Byron Nelson in the mechanics of the swing. Miss

Wethered did not play for too long, but in her short span, she was so impressive that many tried to copy what she did. They may have copied but they never could equal the original. There was only one Joyce Wethered. Just like there was only one "Babe" Didrikson Zaharias.

Who Was Golf's Best Known Lady Player?

There can be plenty of debate about "the best player," but there's no doubt that more people knew "Babe" Didrikson Zaharias than any other player. Mildred Didrikson Zaharias came out of Texas, and in a state that prides itself on the fact that their athletes are special, the Babe was extra-special. She first came to the attention of sports fans in the 1932 Olympics, winning the women's 80 meter hurdles and javelin throw. She also tied to first in the

"Babe" Didrikson Zaharias

120

high jump, but was disqualified for diving over the bar. It was a mere technicality, because it was later legalized. So the Babe had to settle for "just" two gold medals.

The "Babe" then took up the game of golf. She and the game were made for one another. For sheer power, there were few that could match her. But, as the saying goes, "you drive for show and putt for dough." So Babe learned how to play. It was only a matter of time before she won the National Amateur. A little more time and she added the British Amateur title to her list.

Then when she turned pro, she had to beat some of the best to win the Women's Open. There were fine players like Patty Berg, Louise Suggs, the Bauer sisters, Beverly Hanson, Betty Jameson, and Betsy Rawls. Babe won the Women's Open three times before she succumbed to cancer on September 27, 1956. It's no overstatement to say that she was as great an athlete as sports has ever seen.

Who Was the Greatest Lady Golfer?

There have been some really great women golfers. But for me, Mickey Wright has the credentials for that honor. In 1963 as an example, Mickey Wright entered 28 tournaments and won 13—a staggering feat. Mickey is a big gal at 5' 8½" and 140 pounds. The golf ball is no respector of sex, only of power, and Mickey Wright has plenty of that. But don't get the idea that Mickey at her peak was a pounder. She could play every facet of the game with enormous skill. There were those who insisted that she had the greatest swing of any pro in the business. And that included all the men. When Mickey

Mickey Wright, voted Woman Athlete of the Year for 1964.

was doing her thing she had to beat off the challenge of another marvelous player, the big gal from Texas, Kathy Whitworth. If there had been no Mickey Wright, Kathy might head the list. As it is, her credits speak for themselves.

What About Nancy Lopez Melton?

Nancy Lopez Melton has done for the women's tour what Arnold Palmer did for the men. Once she appeared on television the women's tour had a player with charisma. She has a special quality. She has a very wholesome way and while her game is a strong one, there is a great quality of femininity to it. Like Arnold Palmer, she has a great flair for the dramatic. Given the tough situation—needing to sink a crucial putt—Nancy has done it. And while she does not dominate the field as once she did, she has remained a

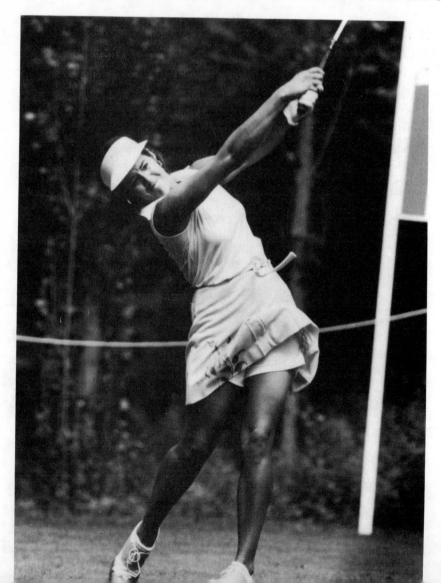

Nancy Lopez Melton,
a million-dollar swing

great favorite. The fact that she doesn't dominate the field is a tribute to the quality of players on the tour. There is for example, JoAnne Carner. When she was JoAnne Gunderson, she was considered the greatest amateur in the history of American golf. She seemed to have it all. No one hit the ball further. She also had great toughness and could putt. She seemed the natural successor to Mickey Wright. It never happened quite that way. Not that Mrs. Carner is less than a great player. It's just that she never came to total dominance. There are other excellent players. Donna Caponi Young, Amy Alcott, Sandra Palmer, Beth Daniel, Jane Blalock and most recently the play of Jan Stephenson. The list of women players currently fashioning reputations for themselves is formidable. It makes one hesitate to single out people for fear that someone might be overlooked. But the desire is not to single out but rather to reinforce the thought that never before have there been so many excellent women players on the tour competing for the largest sums of money ever. Truly they've come a long way.

Wichita's Jim Ryun beating Peter Snell of New Zealand in a mile run.

TRACK AND FIELD

No sport has had as many changes as the area of Track and Field.

Before we get to those changes, just a little speculation on how the sport began. Somehow I feel that's like asking how man learned to do business. "As soon as the urge struck him," might apply. Did Adam suggest to Eve that he could outrun her to the apple? Or did running begin when some man of some ancient era chose not to tangle with some animal and instead decided to outrun it? So we have running and throwing and hurdling and jumping and all of the other things that came naturally. The Greeks, of course, began what may be the oldest of sports competitions, the Olympics. They were held regularly until A.D. 392 when they were banned by a Roman Emperor. At that time they had had a run of some eleven centuries. Did you know that women were not only banned from competing but banned from watching under penalty of

124

death. That's what you really call male chauvinism. But—their day would come. In 1892, a young French Baron, Pierre de Coubertin, proposed renewing the Olympics at a meeting of the Athletic Sports Union in Paris. No one took it too seriously but in 1894, at an athletic congress de Coubertin enlisted more support, and *voila!* the Olympics came into being again in 1896. When I began, I said that great changes have been made, and in so many areas. How shall we begin? Why not start with the event whose winning has enabled a human to be called the "fastest man in the world."

Who Were the "First Fastest" Humans?

If anyone deserves the title, it would seem to be Archie Hahn, if only because he was the first man to win the Olympic one hundred meter run twice—in 1904 and 1906. After Hahn, there were other sprinters like Ralph Craig, and Charlie Paddock, both Americans; the English runner Harold Abrahams; the Canadian, Purcey Williams, and another superb sprinter from the United States, Eddie Tolan. That brings us to the first running superstar, a young man from Ohio named Jesse Owens. In any argument as to who was the greatest of them all, the name of Jesse Owens cannot be denied.

U.S. sprint star Jesse Owens at the 1936 Olympics.

Who Turned in the Greatest One-Day Performance in Track History?

It is generally conceded that Jesse Owens turned the trick at the Big Ten Championships in Ann Arbor, Michigan, on May 25, 1935, when he set four world records in one day. Jesse ran the 220-yard dash in 20.3 seconds, breaking the world record by 0.3; he knocked 0.4 off the 220-yard low-hurdles record with a 22.6 clocking; he broke the broad-jump record by 6⅛ inches with a leap of 26-8¼; and he tied the 100-yard-dash record of 9.4!

In 1936, Jesse set a new world record for 100 meters (10.2) and ran on the American team that set a world record of 39.8 for the 400-meter relay in the Olympic finals. Only three men ever defeated Jesse Owens in a sprint race, Ralph Metcalfe, Eulace Peacock, and James Johnson.

In a world-wide poll of sports experts, Jesse Owens was voted "Athlete of the Half-Century" for the years 1900–1950. He ended his career by turning professional to run on foot against race horses, which gives you a good idea of the professional possibilities open to track stars.

Another great black sprinter, Bob Hayes, ended his career by signing a professional football contract. In 60 races at 100 yards and 100 meters, including five 9.1 clockings at 100 yards, Hayes lost only twice.

Bob Hayes

Who Were the Only Two Men Ever to Beat Bob Hayes?

They were Harry Jerome, Canada's greatest sprinter, and Roger Sayers, whose brother Gale joined Hayes as a National Football League rookie sensation in 1965. Incidentally, after losing to Jerome and Sayers in the same week in 1962, Hayes ran up a string of 44 straight victories (including the Olympic 100 meters) before turning pro.

Another Olympic 100-meters champion had a streak almost twice as long as Hayes'—but not in the sprints. This great hurdler, whose boyhood idol was Jesse Owens, won 82 consecutive races, indoors and out, a feat doubly remarkable because of the ever-present danger of hitting a hurdle and losing stride; there aren't many winning streaks in the hurdles.

Are They Faster Today?

Its strange that in any discussion of great sprinters the name of Jim Hines is mentioned only rarely. Owens, of course, gets first mention; Bob Hayes; the great German, Armin Hary; the Russian, Valeriy Borzov; the American, Bobby Morrow—these are the ones most frequently named and yet when you look to see what is the world's record for the one hundred meters, none of these holds it. That distinction belongs to Jim Hines, whose time of 9.95 remains the record. As a matter of fact, only the Cuban sprinter, Silvio Leonard, has broken the ten second barrier. He ran a 9.98 hundred meters. So are they running faster? My own feeling is if Jesse Owens were running in today's competition, he would beat them all. As an irony, it should be mentioned that when Owens first came on the scene, as great as he was, he still had tremendous competition from a young man named Eulace Peacock. But Peacock suffered a leg injury and that was the end of their rivalry. One other note: it may be that since Hines' record was set at the high altitudes in Mexico City some of the lustre was lost. There are track experts who insist that the record set in Mexico City in 1968 was aided by the altitude.

127

What Other Memorable Speed Marks Were Set in Mexico City?

There were exceptional times run in the four-hundred meter race not only by the winner but by the men who finished second and third. All three were Americans. The winner, Lee Evans, ran for 3.8, which is still the world's record. The second place finisher, Larry James, ran 43.9 and the third place finisher, Ron Freeman, ran 44.4. To show that it was no fluke, these three men and teammate Vince Matthews combined their talents and ran a fabulous 1600 meter relay in the time of 2:56.1, a record that still stands. Also of note was the two hundred meter run of Tommy Smith. He ran that distance in 19.8 seconds. But as great as all these young men were, there is little question that another young American performed to an even greater degree of excellence.

What is Considered the Greatest Olympic Feat?

Most experts now feel that when Bob Beamon went into orbit in the long jump and didn't come down till 29′ 2½″ later, man had accomplished his most awesome feat. The previous world's record in the long jump, set at 26′ 8¼″ by Jesse Owens on May 25, 1935, had stood for twenty-five years! That should give you an idea of what it was like to break a record in this particular event. It wasn't tough—it was well nigh impossible. Then, when it was

Bob Beaman digs his feet into the sand after a record-shattering long jump.

finally broken by Ralph Boston in 1960, the mark went to 26′ 11¼″. Finally, Ralph Boston and the great Russian, Igor Ter-Ovanesyan, broke the 27-foot barrier. The impossible had been accomplished. Could anyone dare dream that 28 feet might some day be leaped? It may seem overdramatic, but when Beamon exploded off the mark at Mexico City and not only went better than 28 feet but better than 29 feet, it was as if time had leaped forward with him. A stupendous and memorable accomplisment!

Who is Carl Lewis?

The obvious answer is an exceptional athlete. The specifics are these: he is one of only three men who have gone further than 28 feet in the long jump. We have already mentioned Bob Beamon, who passed 28 feet on his way to 29 feet. The East German long jumper Lutz Dombrowski also has gone over 28 feet,—barely. But Carl Lewis not only long-jumped a non-altitude 28 feet, 3 1/2 inches, but in the same meet ran the one hundred meters in 10.00. No one in history has run a faster non-altitude time. You might even call Carl Lewis the King of Non-Altitude. Let's turn now to the hurdles.

What Great Hurdler Was Also an Olympic 100-Meter Champion?

His name was Harrison Dillard, and he ran the Olympic sprint instead of the hurdles because in the USA's 1948 Olympic trials he hit several hurdles and could not finish the race. Dillard showed he was a real champion by coming back to make the team in the 100 meters, and then winning at the London Olympics. Four years later, "Bones" came out of retirement to win the Olympic high-hurdles title at Helsinki.

Because the high hurdles are 3 feet, 6 inches high, tall hurdlers have an advantage over short ones, 5′ 10″ being considered the minimum height for a good hurdler. Yet one 5′ 10″ hurdler was as good as they come, winning nine National AAU high-hurdles championships, and carving out his own unbeaten streak of 55 victories in indoor races from 1960 through 1964.

Who Was the Short High Hurdler Who Won the 1964 Olympic Gold Medal in His Event?

Hayes Jones. Jones who used great speed and perfect hurdling form to overcome his lack of height, really "owned" the indoor hurdles. In fact, when he retired he held the meet record in his event in every one of the eighteen major indoor meets. Although he never held the outdoor world record, Jones went on to win the 1964 Olympic Gold Medal in the high hurdles.

But when hurdles events are discussed, no one questions that the names of Edwin Moses and Renaldo Nehemiah should be at the top of the list. Mind you when that statement is made, it is made in spite of the greatness of those such as Rodney Milburn, Willie Davenport, Lee Calhoun, (champion in '56 and '60 at the Olympics), Harrison Dillard and John Akii-Bua. But I repeat, there is only one Edwin Moses and one Renaldo Nehemiah.

What Makes Nehemiah Special?

The time of 12.93. As one who saw the 14 second mark broken and who remembers the greatness of Fred Walcott and "Spec" Towns and who believed the 13 second mark was sacred, I still shake my head in wonder that Nehemiah could have run 12.93. The shame of it is that he and his great American rival, Greg Foster, could not place their names in the list of Olympic champions at this writing. The United States boycott of the 1980 Olympics prevented that. I can't help but wonder: Will someone break 12 seconds?

What About Edwin Moses?

This young man is the dominant track and field athlete of his time. He won the 400 meter hurdles in the 1976 Olympics and only the American boycott in 1980 kept him from an unquestioned victory. That he holds the world's record at 47.13 is no indication of how fast he can run the distance. He simply has never had any rival who might push him to his limit. A student of his event, he has mastered taking only 13 steps between each hurdle and who knows, can 12 steps be far behind? Edwin Moses so dominates the 400 meter hurdles that no other name can be mentioned in the same breath. Which brings us to the middle distances.

How Many Kansans Have Held World Records in the Middle Distances?

Glenn Cunningham, Archie San Romani, Wes Santee and, of course Jim Ryun. Of the four only Cunningham and Ryun ever held the mile record. San Romani's record was for 2000 meters and Santee's for 1,500 meters (the "metric mile"). Ryun also held the record at 880 yards. Cunningham set his mile record, 4:06.8, in 1934. He actually ran a 4:04.4 mile indoors, but it was paced by a quartet of quarter-milers and was never accepted as a record.

Glenn Cunningham

Are Sebastian Coe and Steve Ovett the Greatest Ever?

As of this moment one is tempted to say yes. Consider this. Sebastian Coe has run 800 meters in 1:41.72—an absolutely incredible time. Just think, only twenty years ago the great Peter Snell was running 1:45 for the 800 meters. I can remember when John Woodruff was considered a wonder running under one fifty. Woodruff was a six-foot four-inch man with an enormously long stride and with sufficient speed to run a credible 400 meters. Coe is just five feet ten and weighs a mere 128 pounds. Yet here he is threatening the one-forty time for 800 meters. And that's not all. He has run the mile in 3:47.33 for a world record, and said later that 3:45 was possible. Would you believe that? Interestingly enough, at the Moscow Olympics in 1980 it was Coe's formidable English rival, Ovett, who won the 800 meters, the distance where Coe was considered invincible. To complete this story, Coe won the 1500 meter race at Moscow beating Ovett, who many considered Coe's superior at that particular distance. As of this moment one is forced to add another name. That being Sydney Maree. He is the transplanted South African who now makes his home in the United States and has run under 3:48. And who knows what new face will shortly arrive on the

Peter Snell

scene? It is only fair though, to mention two other names of the past. They are Peter Snell of New Zealand and Herb Elliot of Australia. Snell won two 800 meter Olympic titles and won the 1500 meter crown. He ran under four minutes 15 times. Herb Elliot, also an Olympic champion, ran under four minutes 17 times back when running under four minutes was a feat. Elliot always raced against the best runners in the world and never lost a mile or 1,500 meter race. He had a terrific ability to rise to the occasion. Many track fans feel that a strong finishing kick is the secret of success in the mile. "Give me a miler who can sprint," they say and he'll come home to win.

How Many Men Have Held Seven or More World Records at One Time?

Four: Paavo Nurmi of Finland, Gunder Hagg of Sweden, Emil Zatopek of Czechoslovakia, and Ron Clarke of Australia—all distance runners. Nurmi set his records from 1922 through 1931; Hagg ruled the roost in the forties until he was declared a professional in 1945; Zatopek, a Czech army officer, was supreme in the fifties, and Clarke is still running today.

Who is Don Lash?

Don Lash was the great Indiana distance man of the middle 1930's. Lash, running in the Princeton Invitational in 1936, became the first American ever to hold a world record at a distance longer than a mile, breaking Nurmi's record of 8:59.6 with an 8:58.4 performance. During that period of time, incidentally, another American named Greg Rice of Notre Dame also ran under nine minutes. It was in the 1964 Olympics held in Japan that the United States got its biggest lift in distance running. When Bob Schul won the 5,000 meter run, and Billy Mills the 10,000 meter race it marked a highlight in American racing. I would be remiss not to mention the superb American marathoner, Frank Shorter. He won in 1972 at the Munich Olympics and then was second in 1976 at Montreal. He and Bill Rogers have set world standards in the marathon, an event that had not been particularly

Don Lash taking the lead and winning race.

glamorous to Americans. But the New York City Marathon is a strong testimonial to the impact marathons have had on America. Let's move on to the field events and go back in history to the pole vault.

Which Two Pole Vaulters Cleared Fifteen Feet on the Same Day?

Don Cooper of Nebraska and Don Laz of Illinois became history's second and third 15-footers on April 21, 1951. Bob Richards, the "Vaulting Vicar" who had already cleared the height in indoor meets that winter, didn't join Cooper and Laz with an outdoor clearance until three weeks later, May 11.

Warmerdam used a bamboo pole; Richards and Don Bragg used a steel pole; and although fiberglass poles were being used as early as 1952 (by decathlon man Bob Mathias), the "glass" pole didn't become popular until lesser-known vaulters catapulted to 16-foot vaults by using it. John Uelses made the first 16-foot vault in 1962, and John Pennel first cleared 17 feet a year later.

134

Where Are We Now?

Would you believe—*nineteen feet one quarter inch.* That's what Thierry Vigneron of France has set as the current mark. And even as I write this, the Russian, Vladimir Polyakov has gone to 19 feet, ¾ of an inch, but there is talk his mark will not be accepted because of some technical irregularities. As one who remembers the day when 14 foot pole vault could win a conference championship, you can imagine what a 19 foot vault seems like? Can 20 feet be far behind? Which leads us to a jump without a pole . . . the high jump. And to John Thomas and Valery Brumel.

Valery Brumel of the Soviet Union.

What Were John Thomas' and Valery Brumel's Highest Jumps?

Thomas' best was 7′ 3¾″, a world record when he cleared it at the 1960 Olympic trials. Brumel improved the record to 7′ 4″, then 7′ 4½″ in 1961,

135

cleared 7'5" and 7'5½" in 1962, and finally reached 7'5¾" at the 1963 USA—Russia meet at Moscow in 1963.

And just seventeen years later, in the 1980 Olympics in Moscow, an East German named Gerd Wessig, cleared the height of 7'8¾". You can see that Thomas and Brumel set standards which even today are excellent. There was another Russian, Yuri Stepanov who became the first non-American in history to hold the high-jump record. But there was a storm of controversy that raged around his record.

Why Was Yuri Stepanov's High-Jump Record Called into Question?

When Yuri Stepanov bettered Dumas' record with a 7'1" jump in Moscow in 1957, he wore a special shoe with a built-up sole approximately an inch thick. The German press dubbed it the "Catapult-shoe," and the International Amateur Athletic Federation withheld recognition of the record for more than a year while debating if use of the shoe was unfair. Finally, the IAAF accepted the record as valid, and then immediately contradicted itself by banning the shoe. We have already mentioned the long jump in speaking of Bob Beamon. But before leaving the jumping area let us not forget a great American and a great Russian who staged classic battles. Ralph Boston and Igor Ter-Ovanesyan were great rivals in the field and good friends off it. Their confrontations helped set a standard in the long jump that brought it past even Jesse Owens' marks.

In the triple jump, the Brazilian Joao Olivera has now raised the standard to 58 feet, 8¼ inches to become perhaps the best ever. I say perhaps. The great Russian, Viktor Saneyev was victorious in three Olympiads, an incredible feat. Would you believe that one athlete was able to win his event in four different Olympics?

Who is Al Oerter?

Al Oerter first won an Olympic medal in the discus throw in 1956. In 1960, he won his second gold medal in the discus. Then in 1964 he won his third and 1968 his fourth. What makes the man even more remarkable is that after having passed up the 1972 and 1976 Olympiads, Oerter went into training for the 1980 team. As you know the United States boycotted that Olympiad, and Oerter lost his zeal. But history will record him as the all-time discus man. History too, must record the name of Parry O'Brien.

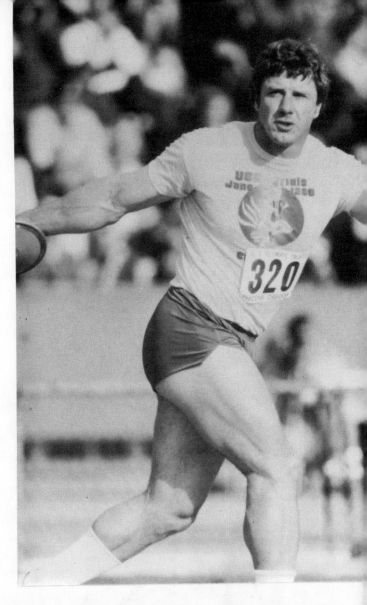

Al Oerter—One in a millenium

In What Year Did Parry O'Brien Retire from the Shot Put?

Most world records are the result of keen competition. But Parry O'Brien was so much better than his fellow shot-putters that over the years 1952–58 he lost only three times in nearly 200 meets. Yet Parry broke the world record in the shot 16 times, improving it from 58' 10½" to 63' 4" in seven years. In May, 1966, the durable Parry won 14 indoor and outdoor national championships in the shot-put, and developed a new style of putting which revolutionized the event.

In 1965, Randy Matson became the new king of the shot-put with a heave of 70′ 7¼″ while he was a sophomore at Texas A&M. Between O'Brien and Matson, though, a couple of pretty fair shot-putters held the coveted world record.

Parry O'Brien puts the shot.

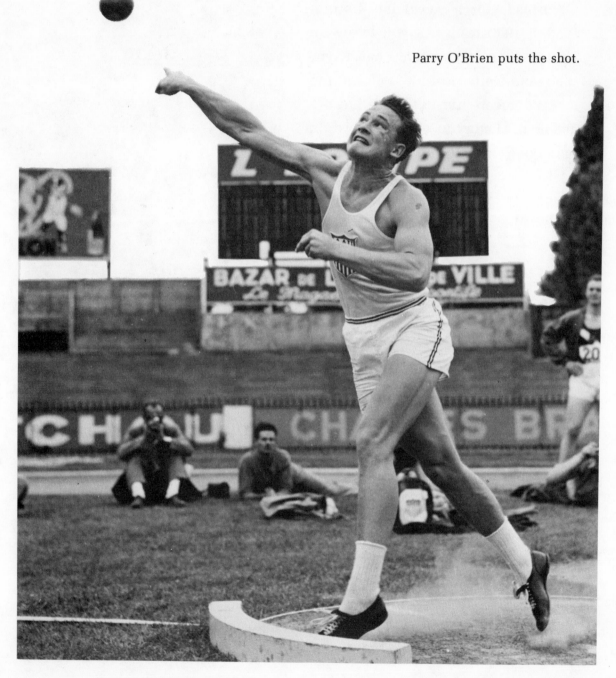

Who Holds the Current Shot Put Record?

The man's name is Udo Beyer. Unless you are really an afficianado, the name may have escaped you. Don't misunderstand because Beyer is an excellent shot putter. His mark of 72 feet, 8 inches attests to that. The big East German can throw the sixteen pound ball.

What Are the Ten Events of the Decathlon?

The word "decathlon" comes from the Greek words *deca*, ten, and *athlon*, a contest. In modern track and field, it consists of ten events, contested over a two-day program.

First day: 100-meter dash, broad jump, shot-put, high jump, 440-yard run. Second day: 110-meter high hurdles, discus throw, pole vault, javelin throw, and 1,500-meter run.

Who Are the Great Ones in This Event?

If I said Bill Watson you'd probably say "who was he?" Well, in 1940 he was the Bruce Jenner of his day. But in 1940 there was a war and so you'll never see Bill Watson's name listed in the Olympic record book.

You will see the names of Glenn Morris, Bob Mathias (he won twice), Milt Campbell, Rafer Johnson, Bill Toomey and of course, Bruce Jenner. All these men won gold medals at an Olympiad. As a matter of fact, so did a man named Jim Thorpe, perhaps the greatest athlete of all time. But they took Thorpe's medal away because he had played in a professional baseball game. He has become an asterisk in the listing of Olympic achievements. Who was the best? They were all great. One woman in track history was as versatile as all these men. In the 1932 Women's AAU meet, this Texas girl, competing as a one-woman team, won five national championships plus the team title. At one time or another, she set world records in the hurdles, the high jump and the javelin and later became the greatest woman golfer of her time.

Mildred ("Babe") Didrikson (far right) winning the first heat of the 80-meter hurdles when she first appeared on the sporting scene.

Who Was America's Greatest Woman Athlete?

She was Mildred "Babe" Didrikson. On that memorable day in 1932 the 18-year old Babe scored 30 points all by herself, while the runner-up team of more than 20 women from the Illinois AC scored only 22 points. Besides winning five events outright, Babe also tied for first in the high jump—with a new world record of 5' 3³/₁₆"!

Who Was the Woman Track Star Who Held Seven World Records at Once?

She was Francina ("Fanny") Blankers-Koen, and although she was 30 years old in 1948, she went on to produce two more world records. At age 32, Fanny set a new standard for the 220-yard dash, and at 33, she proved she was still the world's most versatile trackswoman by setting a new world record in the pentathlon, raising the mark by an amazing 771 points to 4,692 points. That's like knocking 20 seconds off a mile record! But there's more. Today the women are knocking off records as fast as the men. Let me give

140

you some examples. In the 400 meter run, as good a runner as Betty Cuthbert ran 52 flat; it was good enough to win an Olympiad in 1964 and stood the test till 1972 when Monika Zehrt ran 51.08. Do you know what the record is now? The record is 48.6, held by Marita Koch. She would've beaten a lot of men who ran an Olympic 400 meter. In the 800 meters, the Russian Nadyesda Olizaryenko has lowered the mark to 1:53.43. She would have given the great John Woodruff a run for his money at the distance. I tell you, the ladies have come a long way. I vividly remember Greta Waitz astounding the world at the New York City marathon when she broke two hours and twenty-six minutes in that most agonizing event. Her accomplishment has served as a beacon to women who have now had the marathon incorporated into the 1984 Olympics. What else need be said? And yet, there are names still to be mentioned. Wilma Rudolph, Wyomia Tyus, Willye White, Madeline Manning . . . and the list goes on and on.

Marathon great
Greta Waitz

Helen Wills Moody

TENNIS

The game of tennis as we know it today was invented in 1873 by a Major Walter Clopton Wingfield in Wales in the British Isles. It was adapted from the game of court tennis, a game which historians trace back to the thirteenth century. Actually, as in the case of almost every sport, you'll find some who will find origins of a game where no origins seem possible. In the case of court tennis, there have been some theories advanced about the game having been played in Egypt.

At any rate, we know that Major Wingfield invented the game we call lawn tennis in 1873.

142

When Was the Game Introduced in the United States?

The exact date has never been firmly set. A court was built by Hollis Hunnewell and Nathaniel Thayer on Buckingham Street, Boston, on the site that is now Back Bay Station. The year was 1876. This is really the most tangible evidence regarding the first playing of the game in the United States, although there are suspicions that the game was played earlier.

Who Was Considered the Greatest Player of All Time?

Recently I had the pleasure of talking with Don Budge and Bobby Riggs about this question. Riggs said, without hesitation, "the fellow right there—Mr. Don Budge". I don't think he was being gratuitous. Budge, smiled and shook his head, "There is no answer." Don went on to say that in his time he had seen and played against all the great ones . . . Bill Tilden, Jack Kramer, Rod Laver, and has even knocked the ball around with the

A terrific tennis trio: (left) Bill Tilden; (center) Don Budge, about to use the finest backhand in the history of tennis; and (right) Don Laver, the sensational Australian, returning a shot.

modern superstars Bjorn Borg and John McEnroe. He felt that Tilden had perhaps the strongest claim to such an honor because he had been great for so long. He dominated the amateurs for a decade and when he turned pro he was equally dominant. And yet Budge felt that for one point he had never seen anyone so overwhelming as Ellsworth Vines could be. Riggs, in his own right a great player, insisted that what made Budge the best was that he had the greatest backhand and the greatest return of service. Riggs is not alone in his admiration of Budge. Jack Kramer has also suggested that if there is such a thing as the greatest player Budge may be that one. The argument goes on and on.

How Many Players Have Won Tennis' Grand Slam?

The Grand Slam in tennis consists of winning the Australian, British, French, and United States championships. It has been accomplished three times by male players and two women players have also turned the trick.

For the men, Don Budge did it 1938 and Rod Laver did it twice . . . in 1962 as an amateur and in 1969 as a professional. Budge, already mentioned above was born with a great backhand. But his forehand needed work. The results attest to how hard he worked. As for Laver, he was a link in the chain of superstars developed in Australia by Harry Hopman. Mr. Hopman developed Ken Rosewall, Lew Hoad, Frank Sedgman, and Neale Fraser. You add Laver and you've got a testimonial to Mr. Harry Hopman.

Now, what about the two women players who won all four titles in the same year? The first "grand slammer", was Maureen Catherine Connolly of the United States. She did it 1953. Miss Connolly was seriously injured in a riding accident and died in June, 1969, aged only 34.

The second woman to win the "grand slam" was Margaret Smith Court in 1970. Mrs. Court is an Australian. Interesting that an American man and woman and an Australian man and woman are the only players to achieve this unique feat.

144

When Did Open Tennis Begin?

In a historic reversal of policy, the International Lawn Tennis Federation officially approved open tennis at a meeting in Paris on March 30, 1968. Credit for the policy shift was attributed to Britain and its liberal tennis association which had voted to open its own major tournaments to amateurs and pros with or without international approval. The reaction to open tennis was even greater than had been expected. The first open was held in Bournemouth, England, in April. Two Australian professionals—Ken Rosewall and Rod Laver—met in the finals with Rosewall winning 3-6, 6-2, 6-0, 6-3. Laver, considered the world's greatest player, then won the first Wimbledon Open Title by defeating Tony Roche in straight sets. For Laver, it was his third Wimbledon crown. He had won previously as an amateur in 1961 and 1962. Only one other man has ever won three Wimbledon singles championships. Fred Perry, the great British player, turned the trick as an amateur in 1934, 1935, and 1936.

How Did the Davis Cup Originate?

The late Dwight Davis, then a 21-year-old senior at Harvard and an enthusiast of the game, spent $800 in 1900 for the trophy that has assumed his name. He intended the cup for an international competition, to be kept by victorious nations. Under the rules, the nation that wins the cup holds it for a year, then meets the nation that survives an elimination tournament in what is called the challenge round. (Luckily, you can't copyright titles.) In cup play, there are four singles matches and a doubles match. To win, a nation must take three of the five matches.

Which Nation Has Won the Davis Cup the Most Times?

That distinction belongs to the United States, which has won the coveted cup (inclusive of 1980) 26 times. It might interest you to know that among the players who have participated in Davis Cup matches the Italian Nicola Pietrangeli has played 164 rubbers and has won 120. He played 110 singles (winning 78) and 54 doubles (winning 42).

Who Won the First American Open?

This honor fell to the great American amateur, Arthur Ashe. In the face of as strong an open field as could be put together, Ashe, a lieutenant in the armed forces of the United States, defeated Tom Okker of the Netherlands in a fiercely fought final, 14-12, 5-7, 6-3, 3-6, 6-3. As an amateur, Ashe was ineligible for prize money. Okker, a 24-year-old amateur who registered for prize money in conjunction with international rules, won the $14,000 top prize. Ashe collected $280 in expense money.

Who Was the Most Dominant Figure in U.S. Women's Tennis?

Helen Jacobs

Helen Wills, who ranked first seven times and won the singles title seven times, the last time in 1931. Two years later, in 1933, she made a comeback and reached the final with Helen Jacobs. With the score 8-6, 3-6, 3-0 against her, she paused dramatically on the court, walked to the umpire's chair and said with her characteristic poker face: "Please tell my opponent I am unable to continue because of a strained back." There was no love lost between the two stars, and Miss Jacobs, who had won the title the previous year, was to go on to take it a total of four times.

146

What Was the Golden Era of Tennis?

When first the phrase was used it referred to the period from 1920 to 1930 and the illustrious stars Bill Tilden, Billy Johnston, Vinnie Richards and R. Norris Willliams. The ballyhoo over their matches created thousands of fans. In 1926, a match was played that put tennis on the front pages; it was between Suzanne Lenglen of France, called the greatest woman player in the world, and Helen Wills, the all-American girl—calm, cool, and efficient. Suzanne won 6-3, 8-6. It gave tennis a tremendous impetus. The loser became "Our Helen" and "Queen Helen", the biggest drawing card in the game except for Tilden. Then came the four musketeers from France—Rene Lacoste, Henri Cochet, Jean Borotra, and Jacques Brugnon. All contributed to that golden era. Some said there never would be another like it, but they were wrong.

On September 20, 1973 the biggest crowd, 30,472, came to the Houston Astrodome in Houston, Texas to watch Billy Jean King beat Bobby Riggs, over 25 years her senior, in the so-called "Tennis Match of the Century". The millions who saw it on television must have had an extraordinary reaction to the sight. That match catapulted tennis into its newest golden era. And I do mean golden. A few years later when Jimmy Connors beat John Newcombe he received $500,000 for that one match alone. In 1980, John McEnroe earned $1,026,383 and that did not include special restricted events and team tennis salaries. It is a record earn-

Billie Jean King helped start the current tennis boom.

ing for a single year. The women's record, incidentally, is $747,548 in 1979 by Martina Navratilova. The probability is that both marks will be broken. This era with McEnroe, Bjorn Borg, Jimmy Connors, Chrissie Evert Lloyd, Tracy Austin and Miss Navratilova, in my mind is the most golden of all.

Why Are Some Players Better on a Grass Court and Others Better on a Clay Court?

The difference is in the bounce and spin as the ball strikes the surface. A big server has the advantage on grass because his ball skids as it hits, forcing a weak return that he should be able to put away. On clay, his serve is not nearly so effective because the ball will "come up" after striking the surface. On grass, it is dangerous to stay on the base-line because of the peril of bad bounces, so the idea is to get the commanding position at the net as soon as possible. On clay, the movement of the ball is slower, thus making it easier to retrieve shots. Steadiness and patience are required to win a clay match— that is, being able to keep the ball in play from the backcourt and waiting for the right approach to the net. The volleyer is more vulnerable to the passing shot on clay, as the ball will "hang" and allow his opponent time to put it by him.

What Was the Biggest Crowd Ever to See a Davis Cup Tennis Match?

About 26,000 people turned out at Kooyong Stadium in Melbourne, Australia, in 1953, when Australia defeated the United States, 3-2, in the challenge round. Wimbledon, site of the British championship, has drawn up to thirty thousand in a day of play. The Forest Hills Stadium in Queens, scene of the United States nationals, has a capacity of 14,500 which has often been exceeded.

148

Are There Any Small Tennis Players Who Have Become Great Champions?

Yes, Bryan ("Bitsy") Grant of Atlanta, who was in the top ten from 1933 to 1941, except 1940. Grant was five feet six inches tall and stayed on top of the game through his remarkable retrieving ability. His steadiness discouraged his opponents; they could not get the ball past him. He was a master at strategy and in the use of spin and drop shots; he was also a superb doubles player. Another is Ken Rosewall (5′ 8″), the master of control and possessor of what is generally considered the best backhand in the game. An artist in both the backcourt and forecourt, quick and clever, he took over the professional championship from Pancho Gonzalez. Among the present players, Harold Solomon and Eddie Dibbs, "the Bagel Twins," can hold their own with anyone despite their small stature.

What Has Been the Major Change in Tennis Since the Days of Tilden and Budge?

There was more base-line play in those days. Today, a player goes to the net regularly behind his serve and tries to put the ball away with his volley for the point. This serve-volley pattern has been copied so avidly that many fans feel it is producing boring tennis. Yet it is skillful, winning tennis, and, as I said before, as long as it pays off in victories and the rules are not altered, it will continue to be practiced by major players.

What is the Wightman Cup?

It is a trophy donated by the "all-time great," Hazel Hotchkiss Wightman, for a women's competition between England and the United States. The series began in 1923 and is played annually. Three women on each team play a total of five singles matches and there are two doubles matches, making a total of seven matches. Over the years England has won six times and the U.S. thirty-one.

In tennis, as in other sports, the big man has the advantage. But there have been some notable exceptions.

Who Was the Player Who Rose to Fame Despite Having Diabetes?

Billy Talbert. Helped by insulin injections and pills and special exercises, this Cincinnati-born star played for many years in top competition, gaining high rank. Talbert had to modify his game to cope with his ailment. He knew that he would weaken in long matches, so he developed an effort-saving style. For instance, he was famous for his short-swing serve and the economy of his ground strokes. The highest ranking he achieved was third in 1949. He was unsurpassed as a doubles player, winning the national crown with Gar Mulloy four times. He went on to captain the Davis Cup team, although he fell in disfavor with the bigwigs because of his independence. Today he is regarded as the elder statesman of tennis because of his experience and his thorough knowledge of the game.

Do Top Singles Players Make Good Doubles Players?

Not necessarily. The reason is that doubles play requires more varied types of shots. In addition, it also calls for teamwork and special strategy. For success in doubles, the two players must learn to blend their talents so that they may present the strongest front while attacking and defending. Each must be ready to sacrifice himself for the good of the team. The serve, volley, and overhead are the three most important weapons in doubles, and usually the team that is "hitting down," not "up," comes out on top.

Among the great doubles teams have been the aforementioned Talbert and Mulloy; Don Budge and Gene Makop; George Lott and Johnny Doeg (Lott won the U.S. doubles title a record total of five times, twice with Les Stoefen, twice with Johnny Doeg, and once with John Hennessey); Bill Tilden and Vinnie Richards (although Tilden was said to have disliked doubles play);

John MacEnroe does it his way.

Bjorn Borg has been called "the Swedish assassin."

Jack Kramer and Ted Schroeder; John Bromwich and Frank Sedgman of Australia; Neale Fraser and Roy Emerson of Australia; and Ken Rosewall and Lew Hoad of Australia.

Special mention must be made of John McEnroe. Although the young man is but twenty-two years of age and although he has earned great attention for his singles play very little is said about his doubles play considering that he may truly be the greatest doubles player of all time. His matches in doubles have not gotten the exposure that his great duels with Bjorn Borg have been accorded. Experts say that in doubles he is unequalled.

What is the Federation Cup?

It is the women's version of the Davis Cup, originating in 1963. The United States has won it twice and Australia has won it twice. In 1966, the matches were held in Turin, Italy, with sixteen nations competing. The U.S.

151

teams consisted of Mrs. King, Julie Heldman, and Carole Graebner. The American girls defeated Germany in the finals. Australia had been favored, but suffered a setback when top star Margaret Smith was injured and unable to play. The matches consist of two singles and one doubles.

Who is Rated the Greatest Woman Player?

As with the men's section, the debate about the greatest lady player is one that could go on all night. But there is a tendency to lean to the great French player, Suzanne Lenglen. Lenglen was a fiery competitor and a fine all-around player. Miss Lenglen, as was pointed out earlier, beat the woman who is considered by some to be the greatest, Helen Wills Moody, when they met head to head. It could be argued, though, that Mrs. Moody had not yet reached her greatest peak when she played the French star. It could also be pointed out that Mrs. Moody won at Wimbledon and in France, as well as the United States. Strangely, Lenglen never won the American championship.

One factor that is mentioned more today in all sports is that of athletic quality. There is no question that tennis is a "skill" sport. There is a high degree of artistry to it. It's just not a matter of how big or strong or fast you are. If you don't have the skill, forget it. But there is such a thing as being an excellent athlete and for this reason I have the feeling that today's women are as good as any who have ever played the game. Suzanne Lenglen and Helen Wills are before my time but I cannot help but think that Chrissie Evert Lloyd, Billie Jean King, Martina Navratilova and Tracy Austin would have been the equal of any. It stands to reason that with the fantastic prizes being offered more and more women are taking to the court.

Who Are Some of the Other Great Men Players?

It would simply be impossible to talk tennis and not devote time to people like Pancho Gonzales, Jack Kramer, Ellsworth Vines, Bjorn Borg, John

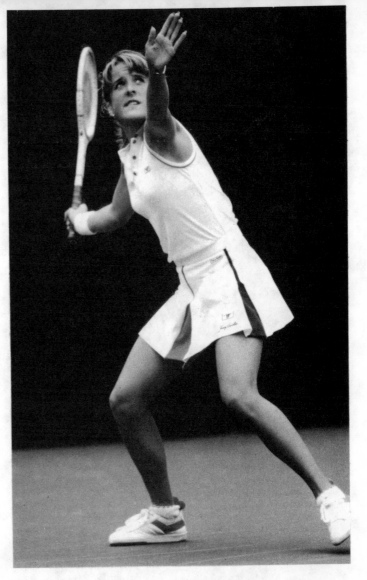

Never too young,
Tracy Austin

McEnroe and Jimmy Connors.

Let's talk first about Kramer, who served the game both as player and promoter. As a player he had few peers and virtually no superiors. He did not have an amateur record to match either Bill Tilden or Don Budge but he won both Forest Hills and Wimbledon and was a key man on the successful Davis Cup Team. When he turned pro he came into his own. From 1948 to 1953 he beat them all on the professional tour. Then, feeling that he had no more worlds to conquer, Kramer turned his talent to promotion. To say that he has done well is an understatement.

His successor was Richard "Pancho" Gonzales, who after having won the American amateur title, decided to take on Kramer in 1949. Gonzales was not up to the task and went down to defeat. But he hit the comeback trail in

Jack Kramer

1951, and by 1954 he was the king of the tour. I mentioned earlier that Bill Tilden had played for many years. About the only man who can rival Tilden for longevity is Gonzales. The incredible Californian was still playing in 1969 and giving almost as well as he took.

There may be some to whom the name of Ellsworth Vines will be meaningless. That's too bad, for when he burst upon the tennis scene, he was a meteor. He hit the ball like it was going out of style. There probably has never been a player who hit the ball harder. From 1934 to 1939, playing professionally, Vines won 257 times and lost 130 matches against the best.

154

The only player to win a majority of matches against him was another great Californian, Don Budge. Against Tilden, Vines won 61 and lost 19, and though the old master, Tilden, was beyond his prime, it was still a considerable feat to beat him at any time.

Which brings us to the three most formidable players of recent times.

Jimmy Connors heralded the beginning of this "new golden age" in a series of matches with Rod Laver and John Newcombe. Mention has already been made of his record half-a-million dollars for one match with John Newcombe. For a burst of time, Connors was unbeatable. Then Arthur Ashe found a chink in the armor when he beat Connors in the finals at Wimbledon by mixing his shots. Everyone up to then had tried hitting them hard at Jimmy and the result was the harder they hit them the harder he hit them back. But Ashe put no pace on his ball and Connors, having to provide that pace, couldn't. More than that, another player had come along to take center stage. His name—Bjorn Borg.

Hit 'em back, harder, Jimmy Connors

There will be those who will point at Borg's inability to win the U.S. Open as a sign of weakness. To me, it is only a sign that he does not rank as the greatest. But he ranks with them all. Not just because he won five straight Wimbledons, or that he was the master in France, but because he may be the greatest all-court player of all time. Equally at home on all surfaces, the Swede has set a standard for both immaculate play and immaculate conduct. In an era where the game has produced terrible displays of bad sportmanship, Bjorn Borg has shown us an example of what gentlemanliness is. For that alone his recognition is ensured.

His diametric opposite is John McEnroe. Few players have ever mastered the racquet as he has. One of his contemporaries has said that McEnroe plays tennis as if it were ping pong. There were moments in his historic confrontations with Borg at Wimbledon and at the U.S. Open when McEnroe reached heights that only a Budge or Tilden had, and he is so much younger at twenty-two than they were at their peak. How great he can become depends more on his temperament than his skill. McEnroe is a better athlete than either Budge or Tilden ever was. John could have been a great soccer player, or even a basketball player. His major flaw has been his temper. It may be true that that temper fuels his drive to success. But seen on television by millions it has served only as a deterrent to the acclaim that would come to him. In spite of it all, he ranks with a half dozen or so men who have made an indelible mark on this sport.